'Dutifulness and Endurance

Bearsted and Thurnham
1914 - 1918
1939 - 1945

Kathryn Kersey

First published in 2005 by Kathryn Kersey

Kathryn Kersey
5 Greensand Road
Bearsted
Maidstone
Kent
ME15 8NY

A catalogue record for this book is available from the British Library.

ISBN 0-9545831-1-6

Front and back covers:
A watercolour study of poppies by Richard Odell, November 2004

Digitally set in 11 pt and 18pt Garamond, 8 pt and 10 pt Times New Roman
Printed and bound in Great Britain by Parchment (Oxford) Limited

Acknowledgments

I thank most gratefully Evelyn Pearce and Margery Gibson for lending the original small booklet concerning Bearsted's contribution to the First World War and several photographs, the family of the late Joy Ferrell for generous permission to use her work on the Second War casualties in Bearsted and Thurnham, Stuart Bligh and all the staff at the Centre for Kentish Studies in Maidstone who coped with a myriad of document requests, the very helpful staff at the Bearsted and Madginford branches of the Kent Library Service, the staff at Maidstone reference library for wonderful assistance concerning the reader/printer machines during lengthy searches of the Kent Messenger microfilms, and the staff at Downs Mail.

I have been able to include many photographs through the courtesy and generosity of the Kent Messenger newspaper group. I thank David Barnes for permission to use information from his website about the Royal Flying Corps and Royal Air Force in the First World War. I also thank Marion and Peter Hebblethwaite for permission to use information from their website about the George Cross.

I thank Jean and John Franklin for generously sharing information, compiled over many months, about George Lawrence and Pamela Thorpe.

Immense thanks and deep appreciation to Richard Odell for his exquisite painting of poppies and for his most generous permission to use it on the front cover.

I especially thank Anne and James Clinch, Michael Perring and Roger Vidler for their powers of general knowledge, observation and detection. I hugely appreciate their quite infectious enthusiasm and companionship during the hours spent undertaking additional research.

I would like to acknowledge the kind assistance, together with permission to quote and use as a source of information and illustrations, the following people and organisations:

Robin Ambrose, Mrs and Mrs Steve Ashdown, Mary Baker, Bearsted and District Local History Society, Bearsted Scout Group, Bearsted Parish Council, John Blamire Brown, BJW Computers, Irene Bourne, Joyce Bourne, Mary Busbridge, the late Ella Cardwell, Anthony Chadwick, Terry Clark, Edith Coales, John Corbin, Theresa and David Elliott, Martin Elms, Audrey Fermor, Alan Ferrell and the family of the late Joy Ferrell, Tony and Sheila Foster, Denis Fowle, Evelyn Fridd, Friends of Holy Cross church Bearsted, Peter Gentry, John Gilbert, Norah Giles, Jonathan Glenister, Joan Harden, Winifred Harris, Jacqueline Holt, Jenni Hudson, Chris and Sue Hunt, Richard Hunt, Brenda Iacovides, Trudy Johnson, Jean Jones, Kent Archaeological Society, the Kent Messenger Newspaper Group, Amanda and Mark Lane, John and Betty Mills, James Moore, Maidstone Museum, Mirror Group newspapers, the late Jessie Page, Rosemary Pearce, Margaret Plowright, all the staff at Roseacre School, Peter Rosevear, Rosemary Smith, Joan Thorne, Thurnham Parish Council, Patrick Walton and Martin Weeks.

Every reasonable effort has been made to contact the copyright holders for Mr Cornford, Miss L Grace Dibble and Thomas Gilbert, but I have been wholly unsuccessful. I would welcome the opportunity to contact the relevant copyright holders in order that formal permission may be obtained for using this information and would be pleased to insert the appropriate acknowledgement in any subsequent re-printing of this book.

I acknowledge the generous financial support of the following organisations towards the costs of producing and publishing this book: The Bearsted and Thurnham Fayre Committee; Bearsted and District Local History Society; Bearsted Parish Council; The Friends of Holy Cross church, Bearsted; The Parochial Church Council of Holy Cross, Bearsted; The Parochial Church Council of St Mary's, Thurnham, and Thurnham Parish Council.

Gratitude, virtually beyond word or measure, is also owed to Malcolm Kersey. He possesses outstanding technological wizardry and editorial processing skills together with unplumbed depths of patience and positive encouragement.

Abbreviations, Symbols and Conventions in the Text

CKS	Centre for Kentish Studies
NA	The National Archives (formerly The Public Record Office)

<u>Latin</u>

Ibid.	In the same place and refers to the previously named publication.
Op.cit.	In the publication already named.
Passim.	Wording used that is dispersed through the text rather than a direct quote.

An asterisk (✱) indicates commemorated on the Bearsted war memorial which is situated in the churchyard of Holy Cross church, Church Lane, Bearsted.

A dagger (✝) indicates commemorated on the Thurnham war memorial or framed Roll of Honour at St Mary's church, Thurnham Lane, Thurnham.

A cross (✛) indicates commemorated on the school war memorial which is a sundial. It was originally located at Bearsted School but was transferred to the current school for Bearsted and Thurnham - Roseacre School, The Landway. An appointment should be made via the school office before seeking to visit this memorial.

Addresses given are all in Bearsted or Thurnham and place names in Kent unless otherwise stated.

For the First World War details, the first date given in each entry is usually the date of volunteering, enlisting or conscription, unless otherwise stated.

Wherever possible, abbreviations relating to military units have been eliminated from personal details for clarity. However, they have been retained where information has been included from sources such as newspaper reports, to preserve the historical accuracy of that source. A glossary of abbreviations used in the source documents is given in Appendix 2.

Contents

Introduction

This book draws upon many records. The First World War section is largely based upon a Roll of Honour prepared by the vicar of Bearsted, Frederick Blamire Brown, in 1919. To this primary source has been added details from the 1918 Absent Voters Roll, and from the war memorials located in St Mary's church, Thurnham, and Holy Cross church, Bearsted.

For the Second World War, the primary source was a list prepared by the Welcome Home committee formed by Bearsted and Thurnham parish councils during 1945. A separate booklet about those named on the Bearsted war memorial compiled by the late Joy Ferrell was also consulted.

Other valuable information has been included – newspaper accounts, parish magazine extracts, oral history contributions, and treasured photographs of family members; some of whom 'went to serve their king and country' and never returned.

As Frederick Blamire Brown once wrote, this book is intended to record the names of all who gave wartime service; those who rendered 'Dutifulness and Endurance'. As the First World War begins to pass from living memory and the sixtieth anniversary of the end of World War Two is commemorated, it is important that the services of the local inhabitants in wartime are both recorded and recognised.

Although it is acknowledged that the record is incomplete, and gaps remain in the information for Thurnham, every effort has been made to obtain full details. However, Bearsted and District Local History Society will be pleased to receive corrections. The more information received, the more accurate and detailed will be the inevitable, future revised account.

It should be noted that the quality of the photographs that accompany some of the newspaper transcripts is variable. The original photographs were produced and printed on poor quality paper that was commonly available for newsprint in wartime. The original paper and corresponding picture quality had begun to deteriorate when it was microfilmed. The microfilm has now been used many times and become worn, further affecting the picture quality. Every effort has been made to achieve a good photographic reproduction.

I have now realised why Professor Richard Holmes, an immense authority on military matters, occasionally gazes upon his garden in a haze of tears. Compiling this book has been an honour and a tremendous privilege.

Kathryn Kersey

First World War: 1914 to 1918

This is the front cover of the booklet giving details of war service rendered in Bearsted compiled and published by the Rev Frederick Blamire Brown, vicar of Bearsted, in 1920. Three hundred copies were printed.

PARISH OF BEARSTED.

Roll of Honour

being a List of those connected with the Parish who served in His Majesty's Forces in the years 1914 to 1919, with some record of their military service.

ISSUED AS

A Tribute of Respect and Honour

AND IN TOKEN OF

The Remembrance and Gratitude

which is due to them for all time for the Victory won through their dutifulness and endurance.

January, 1920.

After war was declared on 4 August 1914, men immediately volunteered to join the armed forces. Advertisements such as the one below regularly featured in the local press. This one appeared in the Kent Messenger, 15 August 1914:

YOUR KING & COUNTRY NEED YOU.

A CALL TO ARMS.

An addition of 100,000 men to His Majesty's Regular Army is immediately necessary in the present grave National Emergency.

TERMS OF SERVICE.

General Service for a period of 3 years or until the war is concluded.

Age of Enlistment between **19 and 30.**

HOW TO JOIN.

Full Information can be obtained at any Post Office in the Kingdom, or at any Military Depot and Recruiting Offices.

GOD SAVE THE KING.

Reproduced courtesy of Kent Messenger group

As a result of the increased numbers in the armed forces, the local regiments rapidly added new battalions. This advertisement, to assist recruitment, appeared in the Kent Messenger, 22 August 1914:

The Royal West Kent Regiment

A NEW BATTALION BEING RAISED.

SPECIAL RECRUITING CENTRES.

IT has been arranged with Major Martyn, the Secretary Kent Territorial Force Association, that all Sub-Committees and Organizations, etc., who are assisting in Recruiting for the Army, should send men desirous of enlisting to the following Centres, where all the necessary Documents and Papers will be prepared and the men fully dealt with, medically examined, etc., and passed to their Units.

1. **MAIDSTONE.** Office in the Barracks.
   Recruiting Officer: CAPTAIN BEECHING.
2. **TONBRIDGE.** Office in Territorial Headquarters.
   Recruiting Officer: COLONEL RATTRAY.
3. **BROMLEY.** Office next to Drill Hall.
   Recruiting Officer: CAPTAIN TOWEL.
4. **GRAVESEND.** Office in Barracks.
   Recruiting Officer: CAPTAIN BAILEY.
5. **CHATHAM.** Army Recruiting Office, Dock Road.
   Recruiting Officer: MAJOR ANDERSON.
6. **SHEERNESS.** Office in Trinity Road.
   Recruiting Officer: COLONEL STALLON, V.D.

It should be impressed on everyone that Recruits are urgently needed for the New Battalion of the Royal West Kent Regiment now being raised at Maidstone.

G. W. MAUNSELL, Colonel,
Commanding Depot Royal West Kent Regiment.

MAIDSTONE, 15th August, 1914.

Reproduced courtesy of Kent Messenger group

ALLCORN HAROLD
Acacia Villas, Willington Road
Single
Parents Thomas and Harriet Allcorn
2 October 1917
Posted overseas 1 April 1918
France April to October 1918
Loos
Demobilised 21 May 1919

ALLCORN REGINALD *
Acacia Villas, Willington Road
Single
Parents Thomas and Harriet Allcorn
29 October 1915 10th (Service) (Kent County) Battalion, The Queen's Own (Royal West Kent Regiment)
Service Number G/10495 Private
Posted overseas 5 May 1916
France May 1916 to March 1918
Wounded
Missing, presumed killed, 23 March 1918, aged 21
Commemorated Bay 7, Arras Memorial, Pas de Calais, France

A transcript of the report from the Kent Messenger, 22 February 1919:

Photograph courtesy of Kent Messenger group

Pte. R Allcorn (Maidstone)
10th R. W. K. R.

MISSING MARCH 23rd, 1918

Could any of the 10th Battalion, 13th Platoon Royal West Kents give any information regarding No. 10495 Pte. R. Allcorn, who was reported missing on the 23rd March 1918. Any information would be gratefully received by his parents and relatives at No. 1 Acacia Villas, Willington Road, Maidstone, Kent.

ALLCORN THOMAS LOUIS *

Acacia Villas, Willington Road
Single
Parents Thomas and Harriet Allcorn
15 December 1914 1st Battalion, The Queen's Own (Royal West Kent Regiment)
Service Number G/5010 Private
Posted overseas 21 April 1915
France April 1915 to July 1916
Killed in Action 30 July 1916, aged 23
Commemorated Pier and Face 11c, Thiepval Memorial, Pas de Calais, Somme, France

ALLEN ALFRED JAMES WHITACRE

Upper Barty
Married
12 January 1876 The Buffs (East Kent Regiment)
Zulu War 1879, Nile Expedition 1884 to 1885, Tirah 1897 to 1898
Ceylon 1909 to 1913
Companion of the Order of the Bath 1908
Rejoined 16 September 1914
Brigadier-General commanding 74th Infantry Brigade, 25th Division
England November 1914 to September 1915
Posted overseas 25 September 1915
France and Belgium September 1915 to February 1916
Commanding Halton Camp February 1916 to October 1916
Line R Lys-Ploegsteert
Mentioned in Secretary of State's Despatch 1917

ALLEN JOHN FREDERICK WHITACRE

Upper Barty
Single
18 September 1909 The Buffs (East Kent Regiment) from Royal Military College, Sandhurst
Lieutenant 16 September 1911
Captain 29 May 1915
Attached Nigeria Regiment February 1914 to June 1916, February 1917 to June 1918
Cameroons September 1914 to March 1916
Nigeria March 1914 to July 1917
German East Africa September to December 1917
South Africa (Hospital) December 1917 to May 1918
England and Ireland 1918 to 1919
Twice wounded
Military Cross 1916 (London Gazette, June 1916)

ALLEN ERIC HUDSON

Upper Barty
Single
22 January 1914 The Buffs (East Kent Regiment) from Royal Military College, Sandhurst
Captain
Posted overseas 22 October 1914
France October 1914 to December 1917
Egypt October 1918
First, Second Battle of Ypres, Somme, Lens, Hill 70, First, Second Battle of Cambrai
Twice wounded
Mentioned in Despatches

This undated photograph was taken in Whitstable, but gives a good indication of the nature of national army recruitment campaigns. Most local campaigns were a series of 'Patriotic Meetings' and the poster shown on the left hand side of the picture gives details of one such meeting. Note also the small boy on the right, saluting behind the soldier.

Photograph courtesy of Roger Vidler

Many men that joined the army from Bearsted and Thurnham belonged to either the Royal West Kent Regiment or the East Kent Regiment. These postcards show the regimental insignias and their full titles.

Reproduced courtesy of Roger Vidler

APPS ERNEST JOHN
Single
Parents Edward and Elizabeth Apps of Thurnham
7th (1st British Columbia Regiment) Battalion, Canadian Infantry
Service Number 227722
Died 6 April 1917, aged 29
Buried in grave VI B 22, Ecoivres Military Cemetery, Mont-St, Eloi, Pas de Calais, France

APPS GEORGE
West View, Roseacre
Married
8 June 1916 5th (Cinque Ports) Battalion, Royal Sussex Regiment
Posted overseas 13 September 1916
transferred to 242nd Labour Company attached to Royal Ordnance Corps
and to 48th Division, Army Service Corps
Service Number 420923
France September 1916 to November 1917
Italy November 1917 to April 1919
Somme 1916
Demobilised 28 April 1919

ASHMAN PERCY ALBERT
Ware Street
Private Agricultural Company, Army Service Corps

ATTWOOD SIDNEY
Sergeant in the Army
Military Medal

AVIS THOMAS
Tollgate
Married
24 May 1916 Royal Garrison Artillery including 307 S Brigade
Service Number 86139 Signaller also Gunner
Posted overseas 13 April 1917
Italy April 1917 to January 1919
November 1917 Retreat, Piave, Asiago
Demobilised 10 February 1919

BAKER ALBERT EDWARD
Cross Keys Cottages, The Street
Single
March 1915 281st Company, Army Service Corps later 122nd Heavy Battery, Royal Garrison Artillery
Service Number 059362 Driver
Posted overseas April 1915 France

BAKER GEORGE
Milgate
Married
1918 3rd Battalion, Norfolk Regiment

BAKER HERBERT
Gore Meadows
Single
September 1911 M (VIII) Battery, Royal Horse Artillery
Service Number 67317 Bombardier
Risalpur, India
Demobilised 17 May 1919

BAKER JESSE
Cross Keys Cottages, The Street
Single
1917 Essex Regiment later 2nd Battalion, Northamptonshire Regiment

BAKER JOHN WILLIAM
Cross Keys Cottages, The Street
Single
25 October 1915 Army Service Corps
later 136th Labour Company and attached to 67th Divisional Train
Service Number 82856 Private
Salonika

BAKER MARK
Gore Meadow, Roundwell
Married
8 April 1916 2/4th Battalion, Norfolk Regiment, Territorial Force
later 1/7th Battalion, Royal Warwickshire Regiment, Territorial Force
Service Number 300003 Private
Posted overseas June 1917
France and Italy

BAKER RICHARD
Gore Meadows
Single
9 November 1915 West Kent Yeomanry (Queen's Own)
later 20th (Northern) Battalion, Rifle Brigade (The Prince Consort's Own)
Service Number 212226 Private

BAKER WALTER EDWARD
Ware Street
3rd Machine Gun Squadron, Machine Gun Corps
Service Number 41447 Private

BAKER WILLIAM HENRY
Cross Keys Cottage, The Street
Single
14 October 1914 No 1 Field Bakery, 27th Divisional Train
also 20th Divisional Train and 160th Company, Army Service Corps
Service Number 038585 Corporal
Posted overseas 22 December 1914
France December 1914 to February 1919
Sergeant
Demobilised 26 February 1919

BALL REGINALD WALTER *
South View
Single
Parents Walter and Ada Jane Ball now at Mid Kent Golf Club, Gravesend
13 August 1915 Royal Navy
Service Number J/43059 Boy First Class Rating
Lost at battle of Jutland 31 May 1916, aged 16, on H M S Indefatigable
Commemorated 13, Plymouth Naval Memorial, Plymouth Hoe, Devon

BALL WALTER
South View
Married
8 November 1915 23rd Labour Company, Army Service Corps later Transport Branch, Royal Engineers
Service Number 507533 Sapper
Posted overseas 6 December 1915 France

BARSTOW JOHN MONTAGU ORCZY
Snowfield
Single
3 May 1917 Royal Military College, Sandhurst
18 April 1918 17th (Duke of Cambridge's Own) Lancers
Second Lieutenant
The Curragh April 1918 to November 1918
Belgium November 1918 to January 1919
Passed into Reserve of Officers 23 April 1919
Lieutenant May 1919

It did not take long for some tailors to realise that there was a market for uniform superior in cut and form to the standard uniform supplied by the armed forces. This advertisement for uniform appeared in the Kent Messenger, 5 June 1915:

Reproduced courtesy of Kent Messenger group

BARTON ALAN HENRY
Parsonage Farm
Married
10 October 1902 Royal Field Artillery
Rejoined 9 November 1914 Army Veterinary Corps
Service Number T390105 Sergeant
Posted overseas 24 November 1914
France, Egypt, Palestine
Demobilised 10 July 1919

BATES STANLEY
4 Mote Hall Villas
Single
Father Mr T Bates
16 March 1917 Training Reserve Battalion France
Second Lieutenant later Lieutenant Royal Sussex Regiment

BATES THOMAS HENRY
Mote Villas
Married
Volunteer Training Corps later 2nd Volunteer Brigade, Royal West Kent

BAXTER PERCY WILLIAM †
Weavering Street
Married
Wife Annie Baxter (née Relf)
Parents John and Edith Baxter, 2 Golf View Cottages, Ware Street
Depot, 12th (Service) (Bermondsey) Battalion, East Surrey Regiment
Service Number 22582 Private
Died 12 December 1918, aged 34
Buried in grave K 438, Wandsworth (Putney Vale) Cemetery

BEER HARRY
The Den, Chapel Lane
Sherwood Foresters (Nottinghamshire & Derbyshire Regiment)
Service Number 92017 Private

BEESTON HENRY
Bearsted Court Lodge
Married
5 July 1918 Royal Navy Sick Berth Rating
Royal Naval Barracks, Chatham
Demobilised 5 May 1919

BENNETT ALFRED CHARLES
West View, Roseacre
Single
Royal Army Medical Corps
Service Number 49334 Private
Demobilised 7 April 1919

BENNETT WILLIAM
Roseacre
Single
9 July 1917 Royal Navy
Service Number J73503 Ordinary Seaman
H M S Chester
North Sea Convoys September 1917 to July 1918
Egyptian Convoy November to December 1918
Demobilised 28 June 1919

BENTON WILLIAM MANSTEAD *
Kulm Lodge
Married
14 August 1914 Chaplain
Second Lieutenant 1915 12th (Service) Battalion, Manchester Regiment
France September 1914 to August 1916
Captain June 1915
Acting Major 1916
Four times wounded;
Died at No 36 Casualty Clearing Station 17 August 1916
Buried in grave II F 12, Heilly Station Cemetery, Mericourt-L'Abbe, Somme, France

A partial transcript of the report from The South Eastern Gazette, 29 August 1916:

THE LATE CAPTAIN BENTON

Captain William Benton, whose death we recorded last week, had a remarkable career of adventure. He started life with some fortune and went into the Royal Artillery. He ran through his fortune and had to leave the Army. He emigrated to Australia, and was getting his living there, when the South African war broke out. He enlisted in one of the Australian regiments and served with credit throughout the war, receiving the King's and the Queen's medals.

When peace came Mr Benton began to take a serious view of life, and took holy orders in the Church of England. He was curate of St Peter's, Walsall, for three years, and then went out to South Africa again, but this time as a man of peace and not a man of war. He was priest-in-charge of All Saints', Springbokfontein, in Namaqualand, not far from the border of German South West Africa, and then from 1910 to 1912 assistant curate at St Barnabas, Cape Town. He returned to England two years before the war, and took charge of the parish of Bearsted during the incumbency of the Rev T G L Lushington.

When the present war broke out, Mr Benton found the struggle between war and peace raging strong in his blood. He attempted to compromise it by going to the Front as an Army chaplain. But he could not be content with a mere 'cushy' job, and resigned his chaplaincy to take a commission in the Manchester Regiment. As a combatant officer he did excellent work, his strength of character, resourcefulness and energy making him a born leader of men. He was soon given charge of the snipers in his section of the front line and organised them most admirably. On being wounded and invalided to England in 1915 he was appointed to organise and supervise an important scheme of scouting and sniping here. In this work, Captain Benton was most successful, his energy bearing ample fruit.

Returning to the Front in February 1916, he was again appointed brigade sniping officer, and fulfilled the duties ably. He was wounded while gallantly attempting the rescue of a wounded man, who was crawling back from the German trenches. He had to lie there for three days. When, at length, brought in. it was found necessary to amputate his leg, but this unfortunately, did not save his life. His loss will be deeply felt by all who knew him.

Our Bearsted correspondent writes:-

Captain Benton was a man who had played many parts, and the story of his life which he delivered at Bearsted from the pulpit some time ago, left a lasting impression on the people who heard it. And his experiences made him a splendid helpmate to men, to whom he made himself most popular by his urbanity of manner and among whom he has been much missed. The deepest sympathy is extended to his wife and young children in their irreparable loss.

MEMORIAL SERVICE AT BEARSTED

For the repose of the soul of Captain Benton, a requiem service was held at Bearsted Parish Church at 8 o'clock on Sunday morning, when many parishioners who formerly worshipped with the late officer as their curate attended. Later in the day a special service of memorial of the fallen also took place at the Church.

BETTS ALBERT
Bell Cottage
Royal Defence Corps

BETTS CHARLES
Bell Cottage
Service Number 22079 Corporal
40th (Fortress) Company, Royal Engineers

BETTS ERNEST
Bell Cottage
Royal Engineers

BETTS ERNEST EDWARD
Bell Lane
Royal Air Force
Service Number 406789 Aircraft Mechanic 2nd Class

BILLS FRANK ALBERT
Ware Street
Service Number 373966 Corporal
752nd Area E Company

BODIAM ALBERT
Milgate Lodge
Single
19 March 1917 4th (Extra Reserve) Battalion, Bedfordshire Regiment
France
Demobilised 3 December 1919

BODIAM EDWARD JOHN
Oak Cottages
Service Number 43757 Lance Corporal
1st Battalion, Princess Charlotte of Wales's (Royal Berkshire Regiment)

BODIAM FRANK HENRY
Lodge Gate, Milgate
Single
1 November 1915 2nd Battalion, Duke of Cambridge's Own (Middlesex Regiment)
later 16th (Service) (Public Schools) Battalion, Duke of Cambridge's Own (Middlesex Regiment)
Service Number 43139 Private
Posted overseas 7 August 1916
France

BODIAM WILLIAM THOMAS
Lodge Gate, Milgate
Single
December 1914 2nd Battalion, Dorsetshire Regiment
Service Number 204506 Private
Egypt
Demobilised 7 April 1919

BOLTON THOMAS HENRY
Aldington
Service Number M/225366 Private
Mechanical Transport, Army Service Corps

BOTTEN EDWARD JOHN
Oak Cottages
Married
4 October 1915 Suffolk Regiment Sergeant
later 52nd Graduated Battalion, Royal Warwickshire Regiment
Posted overseas 1 April 1917
France 1917 to 1918, Germany 1919
Wounded at Arras

BROMLEY ALFRED
Orchard Cottage, Roseacre
Married
30 October 1914 4th Battalion, The Buffs (East Kent Regiment), Territorial Force
later 698th Agricultural Company, Army Service Corps
Service Number 242024 Private
Demobilised 27 March 1919

BROMLEY GEORGE
Roseacre
Single
10 August 1914 81st Field Ambulance, Royal Army Medical Corps attached 27th Division
Service Number 493249 Private
Posted overseas 20 December 1914
France, Serbia and Russia
Demobilised 8 August 1919

BROWN ARTHUR STOKES
Holly Villas, The Street
Single
2 December 1915 2nd Battalion, Coldstream Guards
Service Number 17615 Private
Posted overseas October 1916 France
Sailly, Fregicourt, Somme, Boesinghe
Wounded 1917, Invalided out 1918

A transcript of the report from the Kent Messenger, 1 September 1917:

Photograph courtesy of Kent Messenger group

Pte. Arthur S. Brown (Bearsted)
Coldstream Guards

Pte. Arthur S. Brown, Coldstream Guards, is the youngest son of Mr and Mrs C. Brown, Holly Villas, Bearsted. He joined up December 1915, trained several months at Caterham and Windsor, proceeded to France 10th October 1916 and was wounded 30th July 1917. Both legs were badly hit and the right one has been amputated above the knee. He is now in Belton Park Military Hospital, Grantham, progressing favourably.

BROWN CHARLES HERBERT
The Street
Single
3 February 1916 Royal Naval Air Service later Royal Air Force
Demobilised 14 September 1919

BROWN LEONARD
Court Farm, Thurnham
Service Number 94519 Private
260th Company, Machine Gun Corps

BURBRIDGE HUGH
Fancy Row Cottages, Thurnham Lane
Devonshire Yeomanry

BUSH JOHN
Danedale
Married
September 1898 Royal Marine Light Infantry
Major
Recalled 30 July 1914
Antwerp, Egypt, Gallipoli, Anzac and Cape Helles
St Helena commanding Prisoners Camp 1916 to 1917
Pacific Coast 1917 to 1918, Turkey 1919
Wounded 21 June 1915
Mentioned in Despatches

BUSS ARTHUR HERBERT
Roseacre Terrace
Widowed
1 June 1917 Inland Waterways and Docks, Royal Engineers
Lieutenant then Captain 16 June 1918
Service in England
Resigned 4 February 1919

BUTLER JAMES EDWARD
The Street
Married
July 1917 Royal Naval Air Service later Royal Air Force
Service Number 235857 Aircraft Mechanic 2nd Class

CABLE BERT
Binbury Cottage
Service Number 3341 Private
697th Agricultural Company, Army Service Corps

CANSON EDWARD JOHN
Ware Street
The Buffs (East Kent Regiment)
Service Number 4931 Quartermaster Sergeant

CAPON FRANK
The Lodge, Aldington
Royal Fusiliers (City of London Regiment)
Service Number 58400 Private

CARR ALBERT THOMAS
Roseacre Terrace
Married
6 November 1916 Royal Naval Air Service Air Mechanic 1st class
Service Number F23271
Tanks 1917
H M S President
Demobilised 16 January 1919

CARR ALAN GUS
Kentish Yeoman public house
Married
17 February 1915
282nd Mechanical Transport, Army Service Corps attached 18th Brigade, Royal Garrison Artillery
Service Number 049563 Private
Posted overseas 17 April 1915
Demobilised 9 June 1919

CATHCART DAVID ANDREW *†
The White Lodge
Married
Wife Emma Mahala Cathcart
Children Ewart Aliwal Andrew Cathcart, Hazel May Cathcart
7 August 1900 2nd Dragoons (Royal Scots Greys)

Posted overseas August 1914
Second Lieutenant 7ᵗʰ (Service) Battalion, The Queen's Own (Royal West Kent Regiment)
France August 1914 to July 1916
Acting Captain
Mons, Marne, Ypres, Somme
Killed in action 13 July 1916, aged 33
Buried in grave I D 17, Peronne Road Cemetery, Maricourt, Somme, France

David was born in Ballymena, County Antrim. He had two siblings: James who was in the Scots Guards and John who was in the Royal Marines. Before the war, David was employed by Robert Boal of Co. Antrim. He was sent to a riding school at Canterbury as he was an excellent horseman.

David married Emma Weeks at St Paul's church, Canterbury, 2 December 1909. They shared White Lodge in Bearsted with Emma's sisters. He became a casualty on 13 July 1916, having being pierced by shrapnel, and died without gaining consciousness. Emma Cathcart died on 19 March 1917, aged 35. She had never completely recovered from the shock of her husband's death.

Ewart Cathcart was an excellent cricketer and footballer who played for Bearsted. He died in September 1995 and his ashes were interred in his mother's grave in Holy Cross churchyard, Bearsted.

A transcript of the report from the Kent Messenger, 29 July 1916:

KENT'S TOLL IN THE GREAT ADVANCE

'For King and Country'

Photograph courtesy of Kent Messenger group

LIEUT CATHCART

A fine young officer has been lost to the service and to the West Kents in particular, by the death of Second-Lieut. Cathcart, who was killed in action on July 14ᵗʰ Lieut. Cathcart who was a native of Glasgow, received his commission in December 1915 as a reward for excellent service in the field. He joined the Scots Greys in Edinburgh in 1901, was soon after made Corporal and sent to Canterbury to the Riding Establishment. In the following August, 1902, he left Canterbury to rejoin at Aldershot, before proceeding to South Africa. After he had been with his regiment for a year and nine months, the Royal Scots Greys returned to England. He was quartered at various places until October 1910 when his regiment was ordered to York, where it remained until the outbreak of the war, but between 1910-1914, Second-Lieut. Cathcart passed through the Cavalry School at Netheravon (1911) and the Hythe School of Musketry (1913). He was deservedly considered one of the finest horsemen in the British Army, was a prominent figure at the Annual Military Tournament in London during the past ten years and was the proud possessor of championship medals for heads and posts, driving, thrusting and lemon cutting. He was also the winner of the Sword, Lance and Revolver (combined) Competition (1914) both in the Northern Command and at the London Tournament of that year.

At his own request, on obtaining his commission, Second Lieutenant Cathcart joined the Royal West Kent Regiment in the trenches. He spent his last leave in April at White Lodge, Bearsted. A widow and two children mourn the loss of an exemplary husband and father, whose memory is held in much respect. His Major writes: "Although he had only been with is a comparatively short time, he had won the heart of all, and he is a real loss to the Battalion in every way." A private (his servant) writes: "He died doing his duty, leading his transport to the last. A braver man there could not have been; even when he was so badly wounded, he gave orders for the transport to get out of the danger. He died within an hour of being hit. I could not have lost a greater friend."

CAUSON FRANCIS

41 Mill Street, Ayr
Married
Wife Jemima Crombie Causon
Parents Edward and Williamina Causon, 38 Broad Street, Canterbury
2nd Battalion, Royal Scots Fusiliers
Service Number 9820 Sergeant
Missing, presumed killed, 24 October 1914, aged 24
Commemorated Panel 19 and 33, Menin Gate, Ypres, West Vlaanderen, Belgium

A transcript of the report from the Kent Messenger, 19 June 1915:

Photograph courtesy of Kent Messenger group

Sergt. F. Causon, Bearsted

MISSING

9820 Sergt Francis Causon of the 2nd Battalion Royal Scotch Fusiliers, has been missing since October 24th. He used to live at Ware Street, Bearsted, and before joining the Army seven years ago worked for Mr Montagu Ballard of East Farleigh. He was in South Africa with his regiment during the last rising. His wife is living at Ayr, Scotland while his father, who was a Quartermaster-Sergeant of the Army Pay Corps, is stationed at Canterbury with the Buffs.

CHAMBERS ARTHUR EDWIN

Willington Court
Horse Transport Company, Army Service Corps attached to 1st Cavalry Division

CHAPMAN HORACE †
Roundwell
Single
Parents Mr and Mrs H Chapman, Roundwell
8th (Service) Battalion, King's Own (Royal Lancaster Regiment)
Service Number 23191 Private
Posted as Missing, presumed killed, 13 November 1916, aged 23
Buried in Luke Copse Cemetery, Pas de Calais, France

A transcript of the report from the Kent Messenger, 10 March 1917:

Information Wanted

Photograph courtesy of Kent Messenger group

Pte. H. Chapman (Bearsted)
K.O.R.L.R.

MISSING

Private H Chapman, 23191, 8th K.O.R.L Regiment has been missing since November 13th, 1916. Any news concerning him from any of his comrades would be very gratefully received by his father and mother, Mr and Mrs H. Chapman, Round Well, Bearsted, near Maidstone, Kent.

CHAPMAN JAMES THOMAS
Acacia Villas, Willington Road
Married
1901 Royal Navy
Leading Stoker
H M S Bat

CHAPMAN WILLIAM HENRY
Roundwell
Single
Service Number 156107 Gunner
A Battery, 282nd A Brigade, Royal Horse Artillery
Demobilised 17 April 1919

CHARMAN ALLAN
Ware Street
Mechanical Transport, Army Service Corps
Service Number M2/176677 Sergeant
Military Medal 1918 (London Gazette, March 1919)

A transcript of the report from the Kent Messenger, 1 February 1919:

Photograph courtesy of Kent Messenger group

Sergt. A. Charman (Thurnham)
A.S.C. (M.T.)

AWARDED THE MILITARY MEDAL

Sergt. Charman has been awarded the Military Medal for devotion to duty – saving the guns during the retreat at Mory on the night of March 22nd 1918, and getting ammunition to the battery under shell fire during the great advance.

CHAWNER EDWARD WILLIAM
Ware Street
Service Number 505947 Private
572nd Agricultural Company, Army Service Corps

CHEESEMAN HOWARD GEORGE
Single
Parents Mr and Mrs Cheeseman, 38 Gordon Road, Gillingham
2nd Battalion, South Wales Borderers
Service Number 10441 Sergeant
Died 28 June 1915, aged 25
Commemorated Panel 80-84 or 219-220, Helles Memorial, Turkey

CLARKE GEORGE JAMES †
1st Battalion, Queen's (Royal West Surrey Regiment)
Service Number 3693 Private
Died 25 September 1915
Buried in grave III A 1, Guards Cemetery, Windy Corner, Cuinchy, Pas de Calais, France

CLEGGETT ERNEST ALFRED
Coldharbour
Service Number 2907896 Gunner
Royal Field Artillery

CLISBY JOHN CHARLES
Bearsted
Married
Wife Phoebe Lydia Clisby
Parents Jane Ann Clisby of Ramsgate and the late Samuel Clisby
6th (Service) Battalion, Queen's (Royal West Surrey Regiment)
Service Number G/2829 Private
Died 4 April 1916, aged 26
Commemorated Panel 13-15, Loos Memorial, Pas de Calais, France

COLEGATE GEORGE
The Green
Married
16 March 1916 3rd (Reserve) Battalion, The Queen's Own (Royal West Kent Regiment)
Service Number 12619 Private
Posted overseas 16 June 1916
France June 1916 to November 1917, April 1918 to August 1919
Italy November 1917 to March 1918
Messines, Trones Wood, Hollebeke, Tower Hamlets
Twice wounded Thiepval, October 1916, 27 April 1918
Demobilised 8 September 1919

COOPER ALBERT EDWARD
The Street
Single
27 September 1912 2nd Battalion, The Buffs (East Kent Regiment)
India 1914 Telegraphist
France November 1914
Ypres, Hooge, Hill 60
Corporal
Injured Ypres-Commines Canal, France
Invalided out 10 February 1916

COOPER ALFRED CHARLES
The Street
Single
21 May 1908 2nd Battalion, The Buffs (East Kent Regiment)
Service Number 8874 Sergeant
India and China
France 16 January 1915
Wounded 13 October 1915

COOPER GEORGE HENRY
West View Cottages
Married
The Buffs (East Kent Regiment) 1901 to 1913
South African War
2 January 1917 Royal Navy
Service Number K39354 Stoker 2nd Class
At sea June 1917 to July 1919
H M S Europa I
Aegean Sea, Salonika and Mudros
Demobilised 24 July 1919

In November 1914, contributions were invited for a Soldiers and Sailors Christmas Gift Fund. The fund was the idea of Princess Mary, the daughter of King George V and Queen Mary. The intention was to provide everyone in the armed forces serving overseas on Christmas Day 1914 with "a gift from the nation". Although the contents varied, the box shown below contained tobacco and cigarettes wrapped in yellow paper and some chocolate, together with a greetings card and photograph of Princess Mary. The design of the box lid shows the head of the princess and her monogram.

Photograph courtesy of Malcolm Kersey

During December 1914, there was a dilemma within many families with members serving in the armed forces: was it patriotic or appropriate to celebrate Christmas? One local store offered a practical solution, as this advertisement which appeared in Kent Messenger, 12 December shows:

Reproduced courtesy of Kent Messenger group

COOPER GEORGE HENRY †
Ware Street
Single
Parents George Henry and E Cooper of Ware Street
7th (Service) Battalion, The Buffs (East Kent Regiment)
Service Number 15574 Private
Died 18 November 1916
Buried in grave A 31, Stump Road cemetery, Grandcourt, Somme, France

COOPER WALTER
Milgate
Single

CORSCADEN WILLIAM
Bearsted
Service Number 98508 Private
324th Field Ambulance, Royal Army Medical Corps

COTTERELL ALFRED †
The Queen's Own (Royal West Kent Regiment)
Died 1916

CRADDOCK CHARLES
Bearsted Spot
Married
Salonika

CRICK FREDERICK
Woodcut
Single
October 1915 Royal Navy
Boy rating
H M S Erin and H M S Inflexible 1917

CRICK LESLIE
Woodcut
Single
1918 Royal Navy
Boy rating
H M S Impregnable

CROFT FRED
Bell Lane
Service Number 179403 Gunner
533rd Siege Battery, Royal Garrison Artillery

CROFT STANLEY †
2nd Battalion, The Buffs (East Kent Regiment)
Died 3 May 1915

CROUCHER ALBERT EDWARD *

Bradley's Lane, Roseacre
Single
January 1916 King's Royal Rifle Corps
transferred to 1st Battalion, Oxfordshire and Buckinghamshire Light Infantry
Service Number 23485 Private
Posted overseas May 1916
Mesopotamia May 1916 to March 1918
Died in hospital 18 February 1918
Buried in grave II B 6, Baghdad (North Gate) War Cemetery, Iraq

Albert was born in Hollingbourne and was one of four brothers.

CROUCHER AMBROSE ALFRED

Roseacre
Married
14 April 1915 Army Service Corps Driver
transferred to 4th (Extra Reserve) Battalion, South Staffordshire Regiment 1917
France January 1918 to February 1919
Lewis Gunner
Somme, Arras
Gassed, Demobilised 9 March 1919

Many manufacturers contributed to the propaganda effort. Their advertisements had a patriotic bias, suggesting to customers that purchasing their products would assist the armed forces. This advertisement appeared in the Kent Messenger, in September 1916:

Reproduced courtesy of Kent Messenger group

CROUCHER CHARLES †
Single
Parents William and Esther Ellen Croucher (stepmother)
　　　　1 Leather Bottle Cottages, Little Belmont, Ospringe, Faversham
D Company 1st Battalion, The Buffs (East Kent Regiment)
Service Number L/10663 Private
Died 9 April 1917, aged 18
Buried in grave I N 35, Philosophe British Cemetery, Maxingarbe, Pas de Calais, France

CROUCHER FREDERICK JOHN
Single
Roseacre
April 1915 Army Service Corps
transferred to 3rd (Reserve) Battalion, Prince of Wales's (North Staffordshire Regiment) 1917
Service Number 48779 Private
In hospital January 1917 to December 1918
Demobilised 14 April 1919

DANIELL OSWALD JAMES
Orchards
Married
11 May 1878 50th Regiment of Foot
Egypt, Cyprus
Captain 1885 The Queen's Own (Royal West Kent Regiment)
Major 1893
Medals Egypt 1882, Khedive's Star
Retired 1902
Rejoined 30 September 1914 T/Lieutenant-Colonel
Commanding 9th (Reserve) Battalion, The Queen's Own (Royal West Kent Regiment) 1915 to 1916
Lieutenant-Colonel 1916
Recruiting Duties 1917
Order of St Stanislaus 2nd class
Mentioned in Secretary of State's Despatches, 1917
Demobilised 1918

DATSON CHARLES EDWARD
The Street
Single
1 November 1915 18th Section Field Bakery
Service Number S4 14495 Corporal
Base Supply, Army Service Corps
Mesopotamia

DATSON HARRY WILLIAM ARTHUR
The Street
Single
25 October 1915 Royal Naval Volunteer Reserve Ordinary Seaman
Service Number 3546 Able Seaman 2nd Class
H M S Europa II, H M S Vengeance

DATSON LEONARD SIDNEY
The Street
Single
13 November 1914 Army Service Corps attached to 202nd Infantry Brigade and Base Supply
Service Number S4 238855 Private

DATSON LIONEL PERCY
The Street
Single
16 April 1915 Mechanical Transport, Army Service Corps
attached to 18th Field Ambulance, 6th Division, Royal Army Medical Corps
Service Number 077302
Posted overseas 24 April 1915
Corporal December 1915
France, Belgium April 1915 to November 1918
Germany November 1918 to June 1919
Sergeant September 1918
First, Second Battle of Ypres, Hooge, Hill 60, Somme 1916, Cambrai 1917, 1918 Retreat and Final Advance
Wounded
Military Medal 1917
Demobilised 25 June 1918

A transcript of the report from the Kent Messenger, 2 February 1918

Photograph courtesy of Kent Messenger group

Corpl. Datson (Bearsted)
A.S.C.(M.T.)

AWARDED THE MILITARY MEDAL

Corporal Datson (A.S.C., M.T., attached R.A.M.C.) of Bearsted, has been awarded the Military Medal and Card of Honour for distinguishing himself at Marcoing on the 30th November 1917, when the village was being heavily shelled, by driving his ambulance to and from the advanced dressing station three times, thereby enabling it to be kept clear.

DATSON VICTOR JOHN
The Street
Single
19 May 1916 Royal Fusiliers (City of London Regiment) later Royal Engineers
Service Number 311401 Private
Posted overseas July 1916
Demobilised 19 November 1919

DEAR ARTHUR JAMES
Milgate Park
Married
19 October 1916 Mechanical Transport, Army Service Corps
later 7th Battalion, Gloucestershire Regiment
Service Number 38768 Lance Corporal
India

DENNY THOMAS DAVID WILLIAM *
The Firs
Married
Wife Elsie Mary Gregory of Hill View, Tower Lane (formerly Denny, married 1918)
Father Thomas Denny
Lieutenant
3rd Battalion, Gloucestershire Regiment
Salonika
Died 6 March 1919 aged 28
Military Medal
Buried in north west corner of Holy Cross churchyard, Bearsted

Thomas rose through the ranks and received a military medal for leading the attack against the Turkish forces in Salonika in 1916. He was wounded twice. Elsie was born in London and lived with her aunt at Hill View.

DIBBLE GEORGE
The Poplars
Volunteer Training Corps later 2nd Volunteer Brigade, Royal West Kent
Sergeant

George was Chairman of Thurnham parish council 1943-1948.

George's daughter, L. Grace Dibble, gave a good account of Bearsted and Thurnham during the First World War in her book, No Return Tickets, published in 1989.

DICKENSON CHARLES EDWARD
The Street
Married
1 October 1915 West Kent Yeomanry (Queen's Own)
1916 10th (Service) (Kent County) Battalion, The Queen's Own (Royal West Kent Regiment)
Posted overseas 5 December 1916
France December 1916 to November 1917
Italy March to November 1918
Germany November 1917 to February 1918, December 1918 to April 1919
Messines, Battle Wood, Hollebeke, Tower Hamlets, 1918 Retreat
Demobilised 5 April 1919

DINES F
Willington
Mother Mrs W Dines, of Kingsley Road, Maidstone
11th Infantry Battalion (Western Australia)

A transcript of the report from the Kent Messenger, 12 June 1915

Photograph courtesy of Kent Messenger group

Pte F Dines (Willington)

WOUNDED IN THE DARDENELLES

As already reported in the Kent Messenger, Mrs W Dines of Kingsley Road, Maidstone, late of Willington, has received official confirmation that her son, Pte F K Dines, 11th Battalion, Australian Contingent, has been wounded in action in the Dardenelles.

DINWIDDY MALCOLM JAMES
Bell House
Married
14 August 1901 2nd Battalion, The Queen's Own (Royal West Kent Regiment)
South African War
India March 1914 to January 1915
Mesopotamia January 1915 to April 1916
Prisoner in Turkey 29 April 1916 to November 1918
Egypt 1919
Nasriya Battle 24 July 1915, Siege of Kut December 1915 to April 1916
Major 1918

DOE ERNEST WALTER
Acacia Villas, Willington Road
Single
September 1917 Royal Navy Stoker
H M S Chester

DUNN HENRY CHARLES
Danefield Cottage, Church Lane
Married
10 January 1917 Royal Army Veterinary Corps later 2nd Reserve Section, Army Service Corps
Service Number S E 24928 Private
Posted overseas 29 January 1917
France January to November 1917
Demobilised 11 June 1919

DUREY MARK
Roseacre
Married
22 February 1916 Duke of Cambridge's Own (Middlesex Regiment)
England February 1916 to May 1917
transferred to The Queen's Own (Royal West Kent Regiment) 13 May 1917
Private
France May 1917 to October 1917
Italy October 1917 to March 1918
Prisoner of War in France March 1918 to November 1918
Messines Ridge, Battle Wood, Hollebeke, Tower Hamlets
Wounded
Discharged 4 April 1919

EARL JAMES
Ware Street
Service Number 57328 Private
The Queen's Own (Royal West Kent Regiment)

EARLL BERTIE
Church Lane
Single
18 January 1915 Royal Engineers Signals, 13th Division and 13th Siege Company
Service Number 60575 Sapper
Posted overseas June 1915
Gallipoli, Egypt, Mesopotamia, Kut, Baghdad, Samarea, Kirkuk
Demobilised 8 May 1919

Postcards were a popular and convenient way of communication between families that had members serving in the armed forces during the war; over four million cards were sent. There were many different types available: from simple photographs of buildings, men and regimental mascots to elaborately embroidered cards.

This undated postcard was sent from France and is a reminder of the battles that had been fought:

Photograph courtesy of Brenda Iacovides

EDWARDS CHARLES FRIEND
Parsonage Cottage
Service Number 209049 Gunner
6th Reserve Brigade, Royal Field Artillery

EDWARDS PERCY HAROLD
Roundwell
Single
November 1915 116th (Ontario County Infantry) Battalion, Canadian Infantry
Posted overseas February 1917

EDWARDS WILLIAM TEMPLE
Roundwell
Single
July 1915 Royal Naval Air Service

ELLIOTT JAMES EDWIN
Roseacre Terrace
Single
4 May 1916 82nd Field Ambulance, Royal Army Medical Corps
1918 2nd Battalion, The Buffs (East Kent Regiment)
Service Number 204488 Private
Salonika August 1916 to November 1918
Struma, Dorian
Turkey 1918 to 1919
Demobilised 5 September 1919

This undated photograph shows James wearing his medals:

Photograph courtesy of David and Theresa Elliott

ELLIS BERNARD GEORGE
Home Cottage, Roundwell
Single
Parents May Bennett Ellis and the late Henry Charles Ellis
September 1914 19th (Service) Battalion (2nd Public Schools), Royal Fusiliers (City of London Regiment)
Posted overseas 8 November 1915
France, Festubert Line
Second Lieutenant 9th (Reserve) Battalion, The Buffs (East Kent Regiment) 1916
later 3/5th Battalion, The Buffs (East Kent Regiment), Territorial Force
Lieutenant January 1918
India October 1916 to May 1918, 1919
Mesopotamia 1918
Wounded
Albert Medal 1918 (London Gazette, July 1919)

A transcript of the reports from the Kent Messenger, 26 July 1919 and 2 August 1919:

Photograph courtesy of Kent Messenger group

Lieut. Bernard George Ellis
3-5th Buffs

A MAIDSTONE HERO
The Albert Medal Awarded

Lieut. Bernard George Ellis, the 3-5 Batt. 'The Buffs', East Kent Regiment of Maidstone, has been awarded the Albert Medal for a very gallant deed, which is thus described in the 'London Gazette': 'On the 21st August, 1918, Lieutenant Ellis was with a party at Shahraban under instruction in the firing of rifle grenades. A volley was fired, but one of the grenades, owing to a defective cartridge, did not leave the rifle, but fell back into the barrel with the fuse burning. The firer lost his head and dropped the rifle and grenade in the trench, but Lieutenant Ellis, who was separated from the man by four other men in a narrow trench, at once forced his way past them and seized the rifle. Failing to extract the grenade, he dropped the rifle and placed his steel helmet over the grenade, which at once exploded, severely injuring him. There can be no doubt that his prompt and courageous action greatly minimised the force of the explosion and saved several men from death or severe injury.' Lieut. Ellis, who will be remembered as a keen sportsman, is a son of the late Mr Henry Charles Ellis and of Mrs May Bennett Ellis, of Home Cottage, Roundwell, Bearsted. He is the younger brother of Mr Charles Harold Ellis, and nephew to Mr A J Ellis, partner in the firm of Messrs Ellis and Ellis, solicitors, Earl Street, Maidstone. He thus belongs to an old Maidstone family. His great grandfather, Mr Charles Ellis, was Mayor of Maidstone, first assuming office in 1854. Born on November 21st, 1890, Lieut. B G Ellis was educated at Cathedral School, Salisbury and Montpellier, Paignton, South Devon. At the outbreak of the war he was on the staff of the Union of London and Smith's Bank, Maidstone. He joined up with the Pubic Schools Corps in September, 1914, as a private, trained with them at various stations, including Epsom, and went in November 1915, to France, where he served for six months in the trenches opposite the Hohenzollern Redoubt, and during that period the Germans blew the biggest mine that had gone up on the Western Front at that date. Pte. Ellis returned to England, trained at Oxford, and was given his commission, being gazetted to the Buffs. After being stationed for a time at Dover he went with his battalion to India, and subsequently to Mesopotamia, where he fought in the advanced trenches in charge of his company, and directed bombing operations, in which he had always specialised as bomb instructor to a brigade. It was then that the incident occurred as above recorded. After his gallant adventure Lieut. Ellis was invalided back to India, where he is still serving as captain of the guard to Lord Willingdon, stationed in the hills. Although Lieut. Ellis still carries 350 pieces of the exploded grenade, 77 of which are lodged in his right arm, he is keeping fit and in good health.

The Albert Medal was introduced in 1866. It was devised to be Britain's highest award for bravery in saving lives by a civilian or a military person in acts of great heroism, other than in battle. The George Cross was introduced on 24 September 1940. The Albert Medal continued to be awarded until 1949. By 1970, it was felt that there was little recognition of the Albert Medal and so surviving holders of the medal were invited to exchange it for a George Cross. In 1971, Bernard was one of sixty five people that applied to exchange his medal. At an unknown date, Bernard moved from Kent. He died on 1 July 1979 in Letchworth, Hertfordshire. An obituary was printed in The Daily Telegraph, 10 July 1979.

ELLIS WILLIAM
Egypt Cottages
Married
18 May 1915 14th later 725th Labour Company, Army Service Corps
Service Number 304527 Private
Posted overseas 6 June 1915

FAREWELL CHARLES ERNEST
Oliver's Row
Married
28 December 1902 1st Battalion, The Buffs (East Kent Regiment)
Recalled August 1914
Service Number 24669 Private
Posted overseas 8 September 1914
France September 1914 to 28 December 1915
Aisne, Flanders 1914 to 1915
Time expired; Discharged
Recalled July 1917 8th (Service) Battalion, The Buffs (East Kent Regiment)
France July 1917 to April 1919
Demobilised 4 April 1919

FEAKINS ALBERT AMOS EDWARD
Woodcut
Single
28 June 1918 252nd Divisional Employment Company, Labour Corps
Posted overseas 1 November 1918 Germany
Demobilised 25 September 1919

FEAKINS JOHN
Barty Farm Cottages
1st Battalion, Suffolk Regiment
Service Number 20534 Private

FERRIS JOHN
Maple Bar Gate
Service Number 159682 Private
338th (Home Service) Works Company, Labour Corps

FLOOD JOHN WILLIAM
Ware Street
The Queen's Own (Royal West Kent Regiment)
Service Number 265279 Private

FLOOD WILLIAM THOMAS

Ware Street
2nd Battalion, Queen's (Royal West Surrey Regiment)
Service Number 5318 Private
William was a prisoner of war at Stendal, Germany, from 1915 to the end of the war. This photograph was taken around 1920.

Photograph courtesy of Jean Jones

FOREMAN FREDERICK

Single
December 1915 12th (Labour) Battalion, Duke of Cornwall's Light Infantry
Posted overseas France March 1916 to October 1918
Somme
Demobilised 20 May 1919

FOREMAN THOMAS HENRY

Roseacre
Married
1904 Royal Navy
1915 Invalided
1915 Royal Fleet Auxiliary

FOSTER GEORGE

Church Lane
Single
Volunteer Training Corps later 2nd Volunteer Brigade, Royal West Kent

FOSTER WILLIAM

Rosherville, The Green
Married
26 November 1915 The Queen's Own (Royal West Kent Regiment)
transferred to East Surrey Regiment and attached to 89th Labour Corps
Posted overseas 27 February 1917
France February 1917 to February 1919
Demobilised 27 February 1919

FOSTER WILLIAM

Church Lane
Single
1st Canadian Labour Battalion
Wounded August 1917

FRAZIER ALFRED
The Green
Royal Army Medical Corps

FRAZIER GEORGE
The Green
Married
16 November 1914 Army Service Corps

FRAZIER JAMES
Smarts Cottages, The Green
Single
1910 2nd Battalion, Leicestershire Regiment
Ranikhet, India
Service Number 8933 Private
France October 1914
Egypt 1915, Persian Gulf 1916
Indian Expeditionary Force
9 March 1916 Wounded
Distinguished Conduct Medal, 7 January 1916

A transcript of the report from the Kent Messenger, 13 May 1916

Photograph courtesy of Kent Messenger group

Pte. J. Frazier (Bearsted)
2nd Leicestershire Regiment

AWARDED THE D.C.M.

Pte. J. Frazier of the 2nd Leicestershire Regiment, with the I.E.F., whose home is Bearsted Green, has earned the D.C.M. He had been several years in India when war broke out, and went from that country to the Western Front, in October 1914. He was home on leave in October last and was subsequently ordered to proceed to the Persian Gulf, where he was wounded on March 9th, having meanwhile (on January 7th) won the coveted distinction by saving the life of his commanding officer from destruction by a Turk. He has two brothers in France, George in the A.S.C. and Alfred in the R.A.M.C.

FRIDD THOMAS ALFRED
Roseacre
Service Number 14293S Private
Royal Marines, Deal

FULLER GEORGE
The Green
Married
Volunteer Training Corps later 2nd Volunteer Brigade, Royal West Kent

FULLER GEORGE BETSWORTH
The Green
Single
24 November 1915 Royal Navy Boy rating later Wireless Telegraphist
H M S Conqueror, Torpedo Boat Division
Vimeria
Germany and Russia 1919

GAIN HERBERT LIONEL
The Den
Service Number 111176 Gunner
231st Siege Battery, Royal Garrison Artillery

GATLAND FRANK STANLEY
Milgate Park
Married
27 April 1906 14th (King's) Hussars
India
Reserve 1913
Recalled 4 August 1914 Royal Horseguards
Service Number 47601 Trooper
Posted overseas 5 October 1914
Belgium October 1914
transferred to Machine Gun Guards October 1918
First, Second Battle of Ypres, Arras 1917, Somme
Demobilised 1 March 1919

GILBERT WILLIAM ALFRED
Ware Street
Royal Dublin Fusiliers
Service Number 27531 Private

GILHAM HERBERT GEORGE
5 Acacia Villas, Willington Road
3rd (Reserve) Battalion, The Queen's Own (Royal West Kent Regiment)
Lieutenant

GIRLING WILLIAM SIDNEY
5 Acacia Villas, Willington Road
Mechanical Transport, Army Service Corps

GOLDING THOMAS ASHDOWN *
Roseacre
Single
Parents John Ashdown and Annie Maria Golding
20 December 1914 2nd Battalion, The Buffs (East Kent Regiment)
Service Number G/5230 Private
Posted overseas 28 February 1915 France
Missing, presumed killed, 28 September 1915 aged 32
Commemorated Panel 15-19, Loos Memorial Pas de Calais, France

A transcript of the report from the Kent Messenger, 19 June 1915

Photograph courtesy of Kent Messenger group

Pte. T. Golding, Bearsted

WOUNDED

5230. Pte. T Golding, only son of Mr and Mrs Golding, of Rose Acre, Bearsted, was wounded the head whilst on sentry on May 1st, near Ypres. He served four years in the West Kent Territorials and joined the 2nd Buffs in December, leaving England for France early in March. He is now in hospital at Rouen.

GOODHEW RICHARD
Royal Navy
Chief Petty Officer
Croix-de-Guerre, Italian Order

GOODWIN ARTHUR WALLACE *
Roseacre
Single
West Kent Yeomanry (Queen's Own)
later 11th (Service) (Lewisham) Battalion, The Queen's Own (Royal West Kent Regiment)
Service Number G/7785 Private
Killed in action 20 September 1917
Commemorated Panel 106 to 108, Tyne Cot Memorial, Zonnebeke, West Vlaanderen, Belgium

Arthur enlisted in Maidstone. He is also mentioned on the Otham village war memorial and on a memorial plaque originally in St John's church, Willington, now located in St Nicholas church, Otham.

A transcript of the report from the Kent Messenger, 10 August 1918

Pte. A. W. Goodwin (Otham)
Royal West Kent Regiment

KILLED IN ACTION

Pte. A. W. Goodwin had been missing since the 20th September 1917. His parents have recently received the sad news that he was killed on that date. Joining up on May 24th, he was in England 18 months before being sent to France. He was out there nine months when reported missing, at the age of 25. Before entering the Army he was employed at Sir Louis Mallet, Ward's, Otham and was a highly respected member of the Church Choir for 15 years. His parents, brother and sister wish to thank all friends, for kind sympathy in their sad bereavement.

This undated photograph shows Arthur in uniform:

Photograph courtesy of Jean Jones

GORHAM WALTER WILLIAM
Oliver's Row
Married
January 1916 1st Battalion, The Queen's Own (Royal West Kent Regiment)
later 10th (Service) (Kent County) Battalion, The Queen's Own (Royal West Kent Regiment)
France December 1916
Italy 1918
Germany 1919
Vimy, Achiet, Bapaume
Wounded
Demobilised 27 September 1919

GRANT GEORGE WALTER
Chapel Lane
Service Number 67377 Private
199th Labour Company

GROUT FREDERICK WILLIAM COLLINS
Milgate Park
Single
Service Number 226860 Chief Mechanic 1st Class
Royal Air Force
France

Frederick was Chairman of Bearsted Parish Council 1949-1952

GROUT WILLIAM
Milgate Park
Married
1918 Mechanical Transport, Army Service Corps
Service Number M402491 Private
Demobilised 17 February 1919

GUEST WALTER
Thurnham Court Cottages, Thurnham Court Farm
Married
Army Service Corps

Whilst in the army, Walter looked after the horses. This photograph shows Walter in his uniform, note the spurs on his boots.

Photograph courtesy of Winfred Harris

HAISMAN WILLIAM PREBBLE
Roseacre
Service Number 35530 Private
2nd (Garrison) Battalion, Bedfordshire Regiment

HALLETT GEORGE THOMAS
Ware Street
Service Number 62250 Private Royal Horse Field Artillery
or 622511 Gunner Royal Horse Artillery

HAMPSON DENNYS FRANCIS
The Court
Lieutenant
Rifle Brigade (The Prince Consort's Own)

HAMPSON JOHN NICHOLL
Common Wood
Lieutenant
Royal Dublin Fusiliers

HANNAN GEORGE MADDER *
Major
9th (Service) Battalion, Cameronians (Scottish Rifles)
Died 13 October 1915
Buried in north west corner of Holy Cross churchyard, Bearsted

HANNINGTON CHARLES
Invicta Villas
Married
November 1914 10th (Canadians) Battalion, Canadian Infantry
Sergeant
Posted overseas 27 April 1915
France April 1915 to 1918
Lieutenant 7th (1st British Columbia Regiment) Battalion, Canadian Infantry
Captain Headquarters Staff in Germany
Second Battle of Ypres, Festubert, Givenchy, Ploegsteert, Somme, Vimy
Three times wounded
Demobilised August 1919

HANNINGTON WILLIAM JAMES
Invicta Villas
Married
22 May 1896 19th (Queen Alexandra's Own Royal) Hussars
1897 12th (Prince of Wales Royal) Lancers
Sergeant 1901
Staff Sergeant Major 1912
South Africa, India and South African War
Long Service Medal, Gold Medal of Saint George (Russia) 2nd class
France October 1914 to March 1915
Palestine September 1917 to February 1919
Regimental Sergeant Major 1917
7th Division
Ypres, Neuve Chapelle
Distinguished Conduct Medal, 1914 Star
Demobilised 27 April 1919

HARDWELL WILLIAM ALFRED
Keeper's Cottage, Thurnham Lane
Service Number 38788 Driver
Army Service Corps attached to H & Y Battalion, Royal Garrison Artillery

HARMAN PERCIVAL BROOKS
Rusaker
Single
11 November 1915 Royal Army Medical Corps
Service Number 77128 Private
Posted overseas 3 August 1916
Attached No 31 Casualty Clearing Station
Macedonia and Bulgaria August 1916 to April 1919
Discharged 10 May 1919

HARNETT ARTHUR NORMAN
Otteridge House
Single
Parents Frank and Kate Harnett (née Furber)
22 October 1915 28th (Reserve) Battalion (University & Public Schools), Royal Fusiliers (City of London Regiment)
transferred to 104th Training Reserve Battalion
and 53rd Young Soldier Battalion, Royal Fusiliers (City of London Regiment)
England and Scotland 1915 to 1919
Lance-corporal May 1916
Discharged 1 February 1919

37

HARNETT DOROTHEA KATE

Otteridge House
Single
Parents Frank and Kate Harnett
4 August 1917 Queen Mary's Army Auxiliary Corps Driver
Posted overseas 13 January 1918 to August 1919

Dorothea was one of the first girls from Bearsted to volunteer for military service.

HARNETT FRANK FURBER ERSKINE

Otteridge House
Single
Parents Frank and Kate Harnett
4 November 1914 2/5th Battalion, Queen's (Royal West Surrey Regiment), Territorial Force Private
Commissioned Second Lieutenant 11 August 1915, 9th (Service) Battalion, The Queen's Own (Royal West Kent Regiment)
Posted overseas 31 May 1916
Lieutenant 10 September 1916
178 Trench M Battery
France and Belgium May 1916 to November 1917
Italy November 1917 to February 1918
France February 1918 to February 1919
Germany February 1919
Somme 1916, Passchendaele 1917, Kemmel Hill 1918

A transcript of the report from The South Eastern Gazette 29 August 1916:

FOR KING AND COUNTRY

Mr and Mrs F E D Harnett of Otteridge House, Bearsted, have two sons, patriotically serving King and Country. Second Lieu. Frank Furber Erskine Harnett, the elder son, will be 20 years of age next October. He was educated at Maidstone Grammar School where he was in the Officers Training Corps.

Photograph courtesy of Kent Messenger group

At the time war broke out, he was a pupil in a nursery business at Woking. He was prompt to answer the call of patriotism and in September joined the 2/5th Queen's West Surrey Regiment. He received his first training at Windsor and then came to Tunbridge Wells at the latter...*(next few lines too damaged to be legible)*...on August 31st 1915 was gazetted to the 9th Battalion Royal West Kent Regiment, then at Shoreham, Sussex. He made a speciality in signalling and passed top in the Morse code. He was then sent to Tilbury as an instructor. In May of this year he went to the Front, being attached to another Battalion of the Royal West Kent Regiment. After a good deal of experience of trenches and wire entanglements he took a course in the use of trench mortars and is now attached to a Trench Mortar Battery.

Photograph courtesy of Kent Messenger group

Arthur Norman Harnett, second son of Mr and Mrs Harnett, attained his 17th birthday only last May, yet he is but one inch short of six feet in stature. Like his elder brother, he was educated at Maidstone Grammar School and was also in the O.T.C. there. He held Corporal's stripes and was solo bugler in the band. In October of last year he found the lure of military service too strong to resist and straightaway offered himself for the Public Schools Battalion (Royal Fusiliers) at Epsom, and was accepted. For about four months he was at Oxford, and was ready for the Front when the order came that he was to go to Edinburgh instead. He is now stationed at Holyrood, and though disappointed at not being in the firing line, is content with the duties allotted to him, as every good solider should be. At school, young Harnett won the Monckton Swimming Cup three times. He was only twelve when he secured the trophy for the first time, being the youngest boy who had ever proved successful.

HAYDN ------

In July 1917, it was reported in the parish magazine[1] that Private Haydn was on board the ship Tyndareus when it was sunk, but he was saved.

HAYES-SADLER WALTER

Friningham Lodge
Reserve of Officers, Wa TI Depot

HAZELDEN BASIL

Crismill Farm
Single
11 October 1912 1st Household Cavalry, Field Ambulance, Territorial Force, Royal Army Medical Corps
August 1914 81st Field Ambulance, 27th Division
Service Number 493083
Posted overseas 21 December 1914
Belgium and France December 1914 to November 1915
Macedonia December 1915 to January 1919
Caucasus January to June 1919
Second Battle of Ypres 1915, Vardar, Struma
Demobilised 7 July 1919

HEPDEN GEORGE

Parsonage Farm
Married
10 December 1915 Suffolk Regiment
transferred 1/8th Battalion, Royal Warwickshire Regiment, Territorial Force 1917
Posted overseas 14 June 1917
France and Belgium June to August 1917
Italy November 1917 to September 1918
France September 1918 to February 1919
Demobilised 16 March 1919

HEPTON GEORGE *

Bearsted Spot
Single
Sister Louisa Page of Bearsted Spot
March 1896
Rejoined 19 May 1915 10th Heavy Battery, Royal Garrison Artillery
Service Number 6634
Posted overseas October 1915
Royal Horse Artillery Driver
Serbia, Egypt
Died in hospital 1 July 1917, aged 42, from cancer
Buried in grave D 151, Alexandria (Hadra) War Memorial cemetery, Egypt

George was born in Otham and enlisted in Maidstone

HEPTON JOHN FRANK

Bearsted
Married
Parents Frank and Helen Matilda Hepton formerly of Maidstone, now Colchester
1st Battalion, Coldstream Guards
Service Number 16619 Private
Posted overseas 8 June 1916
France June 1916 to September 1917
Died 22 September 1917, aged 36
Buried in grave VI B 4A, Wimereux Communal Cemetery, Pas de Calais, France

A transcript of the report from the Kent Messenger, 13 October 1917:

Photograph courtesy of Kent Messenger group

Pte. J. F. Hepton (Maidstone)
Coldstream Guards

Pte. John Frank Hepton, twin son of Mr and Mrs Frank Hepton, late of Maidstone and Bearsted, now residing at 42 Hythe Hill, Colchester, has died from wounds. He was born in the parish of St Paul's, Maidstone, and started his education under Mr J. B. Groom, finishing under Mr John Day at Bearsted. He then took up a situation with Messrs Leveritt, Frye and Page, where he served for upwards of four years, leaving there for Surbiton. After sixteen years at the latter place with Messrs Williamson and Co. he left to join the 1st Battalion Coldstream Guards, finishing his training at Windsor where on the occasion of the King's visit to the Castle, he was one of the picked men to form 'King's Guard', a fact of which he was very proud. He left Windsor for France on June 8th 1916, and was severely wounded in the head and admitted to hospital on September 18th last, passing away on September 22nd. Taking up the cause of the Church of England Missionary Society, he was an ardent worker in the parish of St Matthew's, Surbiton, where he will be sadly missed. He leaves a widow and two children to mourn their loss.

HICKMOTT ARTHUR

The Street
Single
24 October 1915 Army Service Corps
Service Number B185514 Private
Egypt, Palestine
Demobilised 21 March 1919

HILLS CHARLES EDWARD

Ty Fry
Service Number 108100 Corporal
53rd (1st) Young Soldier Battalion, Royal Sussex Regiment

HIRST ARTHUR

Roseacre Terrace
Single
4 January 1917 Inland Waterways and Docks, Royal Engineers
Service Number 321658 Sapper

In 1915, many clubs that supported the armed forces, arranged collections of donated items for Christmas gift parcels containing 'home comforts'. These included tobacco, cigarettes, chocolate, knitted socks and balaclavas, which were sent to men serving at the front. There is no mention about this collection in the log books for Bearsted School, but this certificate records a donation made by Sidney Hunt:

Reproduced courtesy of Chris and Sue Hunt

HODGES GEORGE
Ware Street
Parents Harry and Alice Hodges
The Queen's Own (Royal West Kent Regiment)

George reached the rank of Sergeant Major in the army and his service included a spell in India This photograph of George in tropical uniform is undated but was taken during the First World War. Note the Corporal stripes on his sleeve.

Photograph courtesy of Jean Jones

HODGES HARRY
Ware Street
Labour Company

HODGES HENRY
Ware Street
Parents Harry and Alice Hodges
The Buffs (East Kent Regiment)
Private
Badly gassed and invalided out of the army, Henry returned to Thurnham and assisted his family in running Rosemount Dairy farm, Ware Street. This photograph shows Henry in his uniform.

Photograph courtesy of Jean Jones

HODGES WILLIAM ERNEST
The Plantation public house
Service Number R2727 Able Seaman
H M S Perham

HODGES WILLIAM ERNEST
The Plantation public house
Single
West Kent Yeomanry (Queen's Own)
Salonika

This undated photograph shows William Hodges as a young man:

Photograph courtesy of Jean Jones

HOLMES GEORGE WILLIAM VERNEY *†
Ware Street
Married
Wife Gertrude Cecilia Dorothy Tolhurst (formerly Holmes) of Caring Farm, Leeds
Grandfather to Les, Jacqui and Neville
Parents Richard and Lavinia Holmes, Ware Street
2nd Battalion, The Buffs (East Kent Regiment)
Service Number G/4679
Killed in action 3 May 1915, aged 29
Commemorated Panel 12 and 14, Ypres (Menin Gate) Memorial

HOLMES P
Russian Order

HOLMWOOD GEORGE WALTER
Coldharbour
Service Number 226245 Private
692nd Agricultural Company, Army Service Corps

HOLNESS PERCY HENRY
Ware Street
Service Number 63071 Gunner
D Battery, Royal Horse Artillery

This advertisement appeared to give sound advice to families whose loved ones were already involved in the armed forces. It is not clear whether there were shortages by the time the advertisement appeared in Kent Messenger, 26 September 1914:

Reproduced courtesy of Kent Messenger group

HOPPERTON WILLIAM ANGUS
The Mill
Single
31 March 1915 10th (Service) (Kent County) Battalion, The Queen's Own (Royal West Kent Regiment)

HUMPHREYS ALFRED
Roseacre Terrace
Married
Rejoined 6 October 1914 9th (Reserve) Battalion, The Buffs (East Kent Regiment)
later 3rd (Reserve) Battalion, The Buffs (East Kent Regiment)
Service Number S720 Sergeant

HUNT ALFRED GEORGE
Roseacre
Single
11 December 1915 The Queen's Own (Royal West Kent Regiment) later Essex Regiment
Service Number 201586 Private
Egypt July 1916 to April 1919
Palestine 1919
Sudan, Gaza, Jerusalem
Military Medal 1917
Demobilised 15 September 1919

A transcript of the report from the Kent Messenger, 23 June 1917

Photograph courtesy of Kent Messenger group

Pte. Alfred G Hunt (Boxley)
Royal West Kent Regiment

AWARDED THE MILITARY MEDAL

Pte. Hunt, who is a son of Mr and Mrs W. Hunt of Boxley, has been awarded the Military Medal in Egypt.

HUNT EDWARD SPRINGFIELD
Roseacre
Devonshire Regiment
Private

HUNT GEORGE
Ashford Road
Single
1914 18th (Western Ontario) Battalion, Canadian Infantry
France September 1915
Wounded and invalided back to Canada November 1917

HUNT GEORGE
Ivy Cottage
Parents Alfred and Emma Hunt
9 December 1915 West Kent Yeomanry (Queen's Own)
Service Number 528454 Private
273rd Agricultural Company, Army Service Corps

George was exceptionally skilled with horses. During the war, the army put him in charge of two stallions that were on a stud circuit in Kent, Essex and Sussex. He used the stallions to produce a bloodline of horses that were suitable for the war effort.

HUNT HERBERT WILLIAM
Parsonage Farm
Married
December 1917 Canadian Reserve Battalion
Posted overseas 26 March 1918

HUNT LEONARD ROBERT
Ashford Road
Single
1915 35th Battalion, Canadian Infantry
France March 1916
Invalided back to Canada 1917

HUNT RAYMOND JAMES
Parsonage Farm
Married
July 1916 Labour Battalion

HUNT WILLIAM
Ivy Cottage
Parents Alfred and Emma Hunt
March 1915 Mechanical Transport, Army Service Corps, 24th Division
Posted overseas 1 September 1915

This undated photograph shows William:

Photograph courtesy of Chris Hunt

HUTCHINSON ALFRED THOMAS
Fauchon's Farm
Single
October 1915 72nd Field Company, Royal Engineers Driver
Mesopotamia 1916 to 1919
Kut, Baghdad, Persia, Caucasus
Demobilised 1 September 1919

HUTCHINSON HELEN MAY
Fauchon's Farm
Single
29 June 1917 Queen Mary's Army Auxiliary Corps
Posted overseas 15 January 1918
France January 1918 to February 1919
Gassed
Discharged 15 February 1919

There were many national companies that advertised their products as suitable gifts for men on active service and Prisoners of War. These two advertisements are taken from first anniversary of the war edition of The War Budget, 1915, published by the Daily Chronicle:

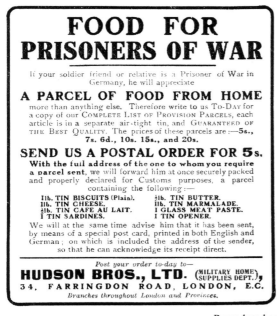

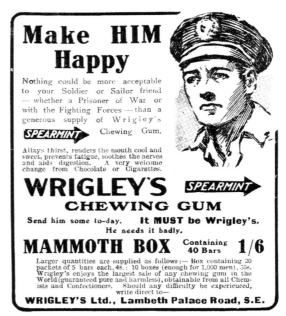

Reproduced courtesy of Roger Vidler

HUTCHINSON WALTER EDWARD ARTHUR
Fauchon's Farm
Single
6 May 1915 Queen's (Royal West Surrey Regiment)
Posted overseas 22 September 1915
France 1915 to 1918
Wounded 11 October 1918
Lance-corporal 5 June 1919
Discharged 28 June 1919

HYDE SYDNEY PHILIP *
Acacia Villas, Willington Road
Single
Father Robert Lough Hyde
December 1914 1st Battalion, The Queen's Own (Royal West Kent Regiment)
Service number G/5024 Private
Posted overseas 22 April 1915
France and Belgium April to May 1915
Killed in Action Voormezeele 30 May 1915, aged 23
Buried in grave I A 10, Voormezeele Enclosures No 1 and No 2, Ieper, West Vlaanderen, Belgium

Sydney was born in Gravesend and enlisted in Bromley.

JAMES RICHARD
Oliver's Row
Married
Volunteer Training Corps later 2nd Volunteer Brigade, Royal West Kent

JACKSON CLAUD
Mote Hall
Single
Army Service Corps
Captain
Lieutenant 65th Training Squadron
Later Royal Air Force

JEFFREY WILLIAM ERNEST *
6 Invicta Villas
Single
Parents Edward and Mary Risely Jeffrey, 6 Invicta Villas
10 August 1914 2nd Battalion, Queen's (Royal West Surrey Regiment)
Service Number G/211 Private
France August 1915 to September 1917
Loos, Somme, Ypres
Missing, presumed killed in action, 25 September 1917, aged 26
Commemorated Panel 14-17 or 162-162a, Tyne Cot Memorial, Zonnebeke, West Vlaanderen, Belgium

A transcript of the report from the Kent Messenger, 21 November 1917:

Information Wanted

Photograph courtesy of Kent Messenger group

Pte. W. E. Jeffrey (Bearsted)
Queen's Surrey Regiment

REPORTED MISSING

Mr and Mrs Jeffery, of 6 Invicta Villas, Bearsted, have received official news that their son, Pte. W. E Jeffrey, Queen's R.W. Surrey Regiment, was reported missing, 25th September. If any of his chums could give them any further information, they would be very grateful. He enlisted on August 10th, 1914, up to which he was a male attendant at Farnham Workhouse, Surrey.

JENNER HAROLD *
Mote Lodge
Single
Parents   Herbert W and Edith A Jenner North Lodge, Mote Park
11 August 1915 123rd Field Company, Royal Engineers
Service Number 38841 Driver
Posted overseas 16 March 1916
France and Belgium March 1916 to July 1917
Killed in Action Yser Canal 31 July 1917, aged 20
Buried in grave I M 26, Bard Cottage Cemetery, Ieper, West Vlaanderen, Belgium
Harold is also commemorated on the war memorial plaque at St Nicholas church, Otham.

Harold enlisted in Chatham

JENNER PERCY LEONARD *
Mote Lodge
Married
Wife Eunice Alice Jenner of Bridge Lodge, Mote Park
Parents Herbert W and Edith A Jenner North Lodge, Mote Park
5 December 1916 594th Mechanical Transport Company, Army Service Corps attached to X Corps Heavy
Artillery later attached 228th Siege Battery
Service Number 273355 Private
Posted overseas 16 January 1917
France and Belgium
Zillebeke
Killed in action 23 September 1917, aged 22
Buried in grave I O 5, Spoilbank Cemetery, Ieper, West Vlaanderen, Belgium
Percy is also commemorated on the war memorial plaque at St Nicholas church, Otham.

Percy was born in Ditton

JORDAN CHARLES EDWARD
Byfrance
Single
August 1916 Royal Field Artillery France

JORDAN ROBERT JAMES
Byfrance
Single
25 October 1915 71st Field Company, Royal Engineers
Service Number 136688 Driver
Posted overseas 12 May 1916
Mesopotamia April 1916 to February 1919
India February to March 1919
Kut Relief Force 1916 to 1917, Capture of Baghdad, Kifri 1917, Kirkuk 1918
Discharged 28 April 1919

JURY HORACE HENRY
Black Horse Inn
The Queen's Own (Royal West Kent Regiment)
Service Number G690 Colour Sergeant

KEMSLEY GEORGE ALFRED WILLIAM
The Royal Oak
Motor Mechanic
H M S Vanguard 5

KITCHENHAM HENRY JOHN
Binbury Cottage
Grenadier Guards
Service Number 25634 Private

LENOISE VIVIAN
Roseacre
Service Number M7373 Leading CC
H M S Pembroke II

LIDYARD JOHN ROBERT
The Street
Married
18 June 1917 Mechanical Transport, Army Service Corps
France July 1917

LISSENDEN ANTHONY JOHN
The Street
1st Battalion, The Buffs (East Kent Regiment)
Service Number 4825 Private

LUSHINGTON GODFREY LIONEL LAW
Cobham House
1st Battalion, The Buffs (East Kent Regiment)
Lieutenant.

MACE LEONARD
Church Cottages
Service Number 92417 Driver
68th Field Company, Royal Engineers

MACQUEEN RONALD BRODIE
Little Milgate
Single
April 1918 Indian Army from Royal Military College, Sandhurst Second Lieutenant
India, North West Frontier 1919
Lieutenant 24 April 1919
Afghan War 1918 to 1919, Musa Khel
Mentioned in Despatches

MACQUEEN WILLIAM JAMES
Little Milgate
Married
1886 Alexandra, Princess of Wales's Own (Yorkshire Regiment)
Major, British South African Police
Matabele War, Mashonaland Rebellion 1896 to 1897, South African War 1899 to 1902
Retired March 1914
Rejoined 16 October 1914 18th (Service) Battalion (1st Public Schools), Royal Fusiliers (City of London Regiment)
transferred to 150th Reserve Company, Royal Defence Corps 1 May 1916
England October 1914 to April 1919
Demobilised 16 April 1919

MANKELOW EDGAR
Willows Cottage, Chapel Lane
Service Number TR 13/77818 Company Sergeant Major
52nd Graduated Battalion, Rifle Brigade (The Prince Consort's Own)

MANNERINGS CHARLES
The Street
Married
September 1917 Royal Field Artillery Driver
France, Italy, Belgium
Demobilised December 1918

MANNERINGS EDGAR *
The Street
Single
Parents John and Malvina A Mannerings, The Street
7 December 1917 4th Battalion, Northamptonshire Regiment, Territorial Force
transferred 1st Battalion, Norfolk Regiment
Service Number 41503 Private
Posted overseas 15 May 1918
Killed in Action Beugny September 2nd 1918, aged 18
Commemorated Panel 4, Vis-en Artois Memorial, Pas de Calais, France

Edgar was one of five sons that served in the army. His parents received a letter of congratulations from the King for this achievement. He enlisted in Maidstone.

MANNERINGS GEORGE
The Street
Married
September 1914 Army Service Corps Driver
Sergeant
Salonika 1916

MANNERINGS HARRY
The Street
Married
September 1914 11th (Service) Battalion, Durham Light Infantry
Sergeant
France August 1915
Wounded 1916
Invalided out 1917

MANNERINGS JOHN ANTHONY
Oliver's Row
Married
25 January 1904 Army Service Corps
Service Number T21788 Driver
later 528th Company, Army Service Corps
Posted overseas 9 August 1914
France and Belgium August 1914 to December 1918
Germany December 1918 to June 1919
Mons, La Cateau, Ypres, Somme, Marne, Lens, Arras, Cambrai, Maubeuge
Military Medal
Demobilised 10 June 1919

MANNERINGS SIDNEY
The Street
Single
23 November 1914 Horse Transport, Army Service Corps, 10th Division   Farrier
Posted overseas 1 March 1915
Egypt March to October 1915
Salonika October 1915 to March 1918
France October 1918 to March 1919
Serbian Retreat, Dorian, Vardar
Invalided out 1 March 1919

MANNERINGS THOMAS
The Street
Single
March 1907 2nd Battalion, The Queen's Own (Royal West Kent Regiment)
India 1909 to 1914
Mesopotamia 1916 to 1919
North West Frontier 1919
Military Service Medal

MANSFIELD FREDERICK
Chapel Lane
Service Number W R/10314
Pioneer 332nd Road Corps Company, Royal Engineers

MANSFIELD GEORGE
2 Chapel Lane
13th (Transport Workers) Battalion, Bedfordshire Regiment
Service Number 39281 Private

MARSHAM FRANCIS WILLIAM BULLOCK
Bearsted Court
Single
1911 19th (Queen Alexandra's Own Royal) Hussars
Captain
France September 1914 to February 1919
Military Cross (London Gazette, June 1916), Distinguished Service Order (London Gazette, June 1918)
Twice mentioned in Despatches

MAXTED WILLIAM SUTTON
Crismill
Single
25 October 1915 Royal Field Artillery
1917 2/1st Battalion, Warwickshire Royal Horse Artillery Second Lieutenant
Lieutenant

MEDHURST JOHN ALFRED
Parents James and Rachel Medhurst of 'The Lord Raglan', Slade Green, Erith
1st Battalion, The Buffs (East Kent Regiment)
Service Number G/10572
Died 19 June 1915, aged 19
Buried in grave B10, Potijze Chateau Wood Cemetery, Ieper, West Vlaanderen, Belgium

From Kent Messenger, 30 June 1917:

For King and Country

IN MEMORIAM

MEDHURST – In ever loving memory of our dear son, Pte. John Alfred Medhurst, the Buffs, who was killed in action by a shell on June 19th, 1915, son of Mr and Mrs J Medhurst of Lord Raglan, Slade Green, late of Bearsted

Sick, dying, in a foreign land
No father by to take his hand,
No mother near to close his eyes,
Far from his native land he lies.

Reproduced courtesy of Kent Messenger group

MELLOR HAROLD
Roseacre Terrace
Single
8 July 1913 Royal Navy
H M S Victorious and H M S Cedric
Ordinary Seaman on H M S Lightfoot
Able Bodied Seaman on H M S Waterhen
Battle of Jutland

MELLOR ROBERT *
Roseacre Terrace
Single
Parents Fanny Mellor of 3 Crisfield Cottages, Bearsted and the late William Mellor
3 November 1914, Maidstone 83rd Field Ambulance, Royal Army Medical Corps, 27th Division
Service Number 497639 Private
Posted overseas 25 December 1914
France December 1914 to December 1915
Salonika December 1915
Lost at Sea in Mediterranean 21 February 1917 aged 23
Commemorated Mikra Memorial, Kalamaria, Greece

It is believed that Robert drowned at sea from the Steam Ship Princess Alberta.

MESSAGE FREDERICK CHRISTIAN *
Single
24 February 1916 7th (Service) Battalion, The Queen's Own (Royal West Kent Regiment)
Service Number G/12309 Private
Posted overseas 4 July 1916
France July to September 1916
Killed in Action Thiepval 29 September 1916
Buried in grave I A 19, Mill Road Cemetery Thiepval, Somme, France

Frederick was born in Yalding and enlisted in Maidstone.

A transcript of the report from the Kent Messenger, 11 Nov 1916

Photograph courtesy of Kent Messenger group

Pte. F.C. Message (Bearsted)
Royal West Kent Regiment

KILLED IN ACTION

No 12309 Pte. F. C. Message, Royal West Kents, eldest son of Mr and Mrs Message, of Rose Acre, Bearsted, aged 20, was killed in action, September 29th. He joined up in February 1916 and went out to France, July 4th, being transferred to the 7th Battalion. Should any of his comrades see this, who saw him at the last, news would be most gratefully received by his mother and dad.

MESSAGE HARRY THOMAS
Roseacre
Single
21 April 1915 2/1 Household Cavalry Field Ambulance
transferred 54th Field Ambulance 1917
Posted overseas 1 January 1917
France January 1917 to July 1919
Beaulincourt, Ypres, Passchendaele, Vimy Ridge, Trones Wood
Wounded September 1918
Demobilised 7 July 1919

MITCHELL ERNEST GEORGE
Howe Court
Service Number 47385 Gunner
Royal Garrison Artillery

MITCHELL LEWIS
Milgate Park
Single
25 October 1915 Royal Field Artillery

MITCHELL WILLIAM GORDON
The Green
Married
20 September 1915 Royal Army Veterinary Corps
Service Number 1385 Sergeant
TTO 67th Ammunition Column, Royal Field Artillery
North Russia October 1918 to August 1919
Demobilised September 26 1919

MOON EDMUND
The Street
Single
19 October 1916 3/4th Battalion, Queen's (Royal West Surrey Regiment), Territorial Force
Service Number 202852 Private
Posted overseas 30 May 1917 France
Wounded severely August 1917
Invalided out 14 December 1918

This photograph shows Edmund whilst undergoing rehabilitation for injuries received during the war. He lost part of a leg and the heel of the other when a shell exploded nearby. He is wearing a uniform that became known as 'hospital blues':

Photograph courtesy of John Mills

MOON FREDERICK WILLIAM
Colegate Cottages
Single
6 January 1915 Army Service Corps attached to 76th Brigade, Royal Field Artillery
Service Number 041194 Private
463rd Company Army Service Company
Posted overseas 29 July 1915

MOORE THOMAS
Crisfield Cottages
Married
September 1914 8th (Service) Battalion, The Queen's Own (Royal West Kent Regiment)
Service Number 718 Private
Posted overseas 30 September 1915

MORGAN ARTHUR
Thurnham
Service Number 13055 Private
426th Agricultural Company, Army Service Corps

NAYLOR FREDERICK
The Street
Single
June 1918 52nd Graduated Battalion, Duke of Cambridge's Own (Middlesex Regiment)
Signaller
Germany 1919

OTTAWAY ALFRED GEORGE
Frininghram
Service Number 107948 Private
50th Battalion, Machine Gun Corps

OVENDEN ARTHUR GEORGE
Romney's Hill
Single
1 March 1915 11th Canadian Mounted Regiment
Wounded
Invalided to Canada 1918

OVENDEN GEORGE
The Homestead, Romney's Hill
Married
London Air Defences 1917, London Electrical Engineers
28 June 1917 22nd Company, Royal Engineers
Service Number 299813 Sapper
Posted overseas 28 July 1918
France July 1918 to March 1919
Demobilised 16 April 1919

OVENDEN HERBERT
Romney's Hill
Single
19 September 1914 West Kent Yeomanry (Queen's Own)
Prisoner of War 1918

OVENDEN JOHN
Romney's Hill
Married
5 April 1918 Royal Marine Engineers Sapper
Demobilised 25 November 1918

OVENDEN ------
Romney's Hill
Single
Women's Army Auxiliary Corps

This postcard is undated but is typical of the propaganda produced. It shows two soldiers about to fight. The encounter was probably deliberately staged, hence the two soldiers flanking the scene with bayonets over their shoulders.

Photograph courtesy of John Mills

PAGE ALBERT WILLIAM *

Bearsted Spot
Single
Parents Albert and Louisa Page of Bearsted Spot
14 June 1915 The Queen's Own (Royal West Kent Regiment)
Service Number 8513 Private
Posted overseas 6 January 1917 France
Killed in Action 16 September 1917, aged 18
Buried in grave G VI A 28, Duisans British Cemetery Etrun, Pas de Calais, France

Note: Louisa also lost a brother during the war – see the entry for George Hepton.

A transcript of the report from the Kent Messenger, 22 September 1917:

BEARSTED

SAD NEWS – Mr Albert Page, of Bearsted Spot, who has worked at Messrs Fremlin's Brewery, Maidstone for many years, received news early this week that his son, Pte. Bert Page, Royal West Kent Regiment, formerly a servant in the household of Sir Reginald MacLeod at Vinters Park, has been badly wounded. The family were expecting him on Wednesday but instead of his arrival they had the sad intelligence that the poor lad, who was only about 19, had succumbed. Much sympathy goes out to the bereaved family.

Reproduced courtesy of Kent Messenger group

PAGE ALFRED

Acacia Villas, Willington Road
Single
March 1915 12th Labour Company, Army Service Corps
Lance-corporal
Posted overseas March 1915

Shops regularly used advertisements in the local press to emphasise that their garments were suitable for war work. This one appeared in the Kent Messenger, 2 June 1917:

Reproduced courtesy of Kent Messenger group

This undated photograph was taken of land girls during the First World War working at Chapel Lane farm, Thurnham:

Photograph courtesy of Tony and Sheila Foster

PAGE FRANK

Acacia Villas, Willington Road
Single
9 October 1916 Royal Navy
Persian Gulf
Demobilised June 1919

PAGE HENRY

Acacia Villas, Willington Road
Single
26 October 1914 Princess Charlotte of Wales's (Royal Berkshire Regiment) later Royal Defence Corps
Demobilised 15 February 1919

PAGE THOMAS FRANK

Acacia Villas, Willington Road
Royal Navy H M S Juno
Service Number K36933 Stoker 2nd Class

PANKHURST BERNARD WILLIAM

North Gate, Friningham
Service Number SS 1011 Sergeant
Army Service Corps

PANKHURST WILLIAM JOHN

Red Lodge, Friningham
Service Number 68651 Private
24th (Service) Battalion (2nd Sportsman's), Royal Fusiliers (City of London Regiment)

PARKES CHARLES DAVID

Parsonage Farm
Married
3 November 1904 14th (King's) Hussars also 20th Hussars
Posted overseas 12 August 1914
France and Belgium 1914 to 1915
Mons, Marne
Wounded
Invalided out 9 April 1916

PAULL JOHN

Shaw's Cottages
Single
13 October 1915 Army Ordnance Corps
Posted overseas 18 May 1916
Salonika May 1916
Demobilised 14 August 1919

PENFOLD GEORGE HENRY †

Station House
Married
Wife Kathleen Agate Penfold
Father George Penfold of Southborough
Royal Navy H M S Hawke
Service Number 164841 Chief Petty Officer
Died 15 October 1914, aged 37
Commemorated Chatham Naval Memorial

PERRIN ALBERT SIDNEY
Woodbury
Married
Volunteer Training Corps later 2nd Volunteer Brigade, Royal West Kent

PLAYFOOT FREDERICK
Triangle Cottage
Single
April 1902 Royal Navy Petty Officer
H M S Vanguard

PLAYFOOT GEORGE
Invicta Villas
Married
Suffolk Regiment

POLLARD ARTHUR
Invicta Villas
Single
12 December 1914 Army Service Corps
Service Number S 4/036160 Corporal
24th Lines of Communication (Supply) Company
Egypt September 1915
Demobilised 7 July 1919

POLLARD CHARLES
Invicta Villas
Single
14 December 1914 Royal Engineers Driver
Posted overseas September 1915

POLLARD FREDERICK
Invicta Villas
Single
10 December 1914 Army Service Corps
Service Number A202195 Driver
12th (County of London) Battalion, London Regiment (The Rangers), Territorial Force
also attached to 1st Battalion, Prince Albert's (Somerset Light Infantry)
Posted overseas 10 December 1914

POLLARD JAMES EDWIN
Aldington Cottages
Service Number 496646 Private
697th Agricultural Company, Army Service Corps

POLLARD LEONARD
Invicta Villas
Single
10 December 1914 Army Service Corps Driver
Service Number T3 029142 Private
Posted overseas December 1914
Demobilised 28 April 1919

POLLARD PERCY
Invicta Villas
Single
9 November 1915 Army Service Corps
Service Number 145661 Driver
Posted overseas January 1916

POLLARD VICTOR
Invicta Villas
Single
November 1915 Mechanical Transport, Army Service Corps
Service Number 148862
Salonika

An undated and unsourced press cutting:

BEARSTED

WAR NEWS

Mr William Pollard, senior, has now seven out of his eight sons serving with his Majesty's Forces and says: ' So would I be, too, if they would have me!'

Arthur Brown, youngest son of Mr Brown, of Holly Villa, Bearsted, was wounded in both legs, and has had the right one amputated below the knee. The left knee is going on well and he is in hospital in Lincolnshire.

Stanley Bates Royal Flying Corps, son of Mr T H Bates, is home on leave, and is about to undergo a course with the Officers Training College at Farnborough in the hope of taking up a commission.

Percy Watkins Army Service Corps, one of the six serving sons of Mr Alfred Watkins is home on leave after 20 months in France, and **Herbert Raggett** is home in the kilt and sporran of the London Scottish.

George Hunt, a driver and military horse-breaker, is also here, and **William Rowland,** a driver in the Royal Engineers, has just turned up unexpectedly, after recovery from wounds and promotion to Lance Corporal.

Reproduced courtesy of Jean Jones

POTTER HARRY
Romney's Hill
Married
15 November 1915 Mechanical Transport, Army Service Corps
Staff Car Driver General Headquarters and III Corps Headquarters
France and Belgium August 1916 to 1919
Cambrai, St Quentin, La Fere, Amiens, Lille, Albert, Tournai
Demobilised August 1919

POULTENEY ------
Roseacre
Married

POUND HENRY SAMUEL
Ware Street
1st Battalion, King's Royal Rifle Corps

PRESLAND THOMAS
5 Mote Hall Villas
Widower
February 1886 Royal Navy Able Seaman
Royal Fleet Reserve 1903 to 1914
Rejoined 2 August 1914
Service Number 136322 Able Seaman
H M S Victorious
North Sea 1914 to 1915
Admiralty Office Chatham April 1915 to February 1919
Demobilised 16 February 1919

PRESLAND THOMAS
Mote Villas
Single
March 1918 Royal Navy Armoury Mate
H M S Dragon 1919

RAGGETT HERBERT EDWARD
The Green
Married
July 1917 1/14th (County of London) Battalion, London Regiment (London Scottish), Territorial Force
later 697th Labour Company
Service Number 517070 Private
France November 1917 to April 1918
Cambrai, Oppywood
Gassed
Demobilised 15 September 1919

READY MICHAEL
Crisfield Cottage
Service Number 66396 Private
186th Labour Company

Many men serving in the armed forces sent embroidered cards bearing patriotic designs to their loved ones. The card below is fairly elaborate as it has both a pocket and embroidered flap. The pocket still has a small card inside it which says 'A Kiss From France'. The whole card is intended to remind the recipient of the loved one, who is absent undertaking a patriotic duty by serving his country.

Reproduced courtesy of Brenda Iacovides

RICE FRANK
Triangle Cottages
Single
7 October 1916 2/6th (Cyclist) Battalion, Suffolk Regiment, Territorial Force
Service Number 265815 Private
Lance-corporal
Invalided out 18 December 1918

RICE GEORGE
Triangle Cottages
Married
August 1914 24th (County of London) Battalion, London Regiment (The Queen's), Territorial Force
Transport

RICE THOMAS MERRALL
Triangle Cottages
Married
Wife Annie Rice, 4 Locket Road, Wealdstone, Harrow
One son
Parents Mr and Mrs Rice, Triangle Cottages
Service Number 514487 Private
14th (County of London) Battalion, London Regiment (London Scottish), Territorial Force
Gassed
Died 15 January 1920, aged 26
Buried in north west corner of Holy Cross churchyard, Bearsted

A transcript of the report from the Kent Messenger, 24 January 1920:

Photograph courtesy of Kent Messenger group

Pte. T M Rice (Bearsted)
Late 14th London Scottish

DIED JANUARY 15TH, AGED 26

The village of Bearsted was impressively touched on Monday by the military funeral obsequies which attended the last tokens of respect and honour to Private Thomas Merrall Rice of Triangle Cottages, Bearsted, who passed away at Hollingbourne on Thursday last. The deceased, who was only 26 years of age, was gassed, during the Great War, in which he served with the 14th London Scottish Regiment, and after being demobbed was never able to follow any employment. He was married and leaves a sorrowing widow and one little son. He was buried near his father, who recently predeceased him, in Bearsted Churchyard. A gun carriage from Chatham conveyed the coffin, covered by a Union Jack and surmounted by deceased's sporran and other military accoutrements and a firing party and a couple of buglers attended from the Maidstone Barracks. The vicar, the Rev F J Blamire Brown conducted the service. There was a large gathering of villagers. After the committal, the impressive sounding of The Last Post by the buglers was followed by the firing of the usual three volleys. Among those present were – Mrs T M Rice (widow); Mrs W Rice (mother); Messrs H F L A and F Rice (brothers); Miss G Rice and Mrs Hughes (sisters); Mrs Rix (mother in law); Mrs Fred Rix (sister in law); Mr and Mrs William Walkling (uncle and aunt); Mr B Walkling (cousin); Mr Apps, Mrs Rolf, Mr Raggett (late of the London Scottish). Beautiful floral tributes were sent by: His little son; his loving wife; his loving mother and sister; brother and sister Harry and Ethel; brothers Fred, Frank, Len and Albert, his brothers; Will and Arthur and Hack (abroad); brother Charlie; sister Emma; Mrs Rix; brother in law; brother and sister in law; nephew, brother and sister; Oswald Higgins; Mrs Deakins; Mr C Brooke Wright; (Turkey Court), Miss D Hills; Mr Apps and friends at Hollingbourne, nephews; uncle and aunt and family.

RIXON BERT
Roundwell
Single
1914 Royal Naval Reserve
H M S Bacchante, H M S Chester and H M S Pembroke

RIXON CHARLES
Roundwell
Married
21 January 1910 The Buffs (East Kent Regiment)
transferred to Machine Gun Corps February 1916
Service Number 28397 Sergeant
Posted overseas 17 March 1916
France March to October 1916
Wounded at Somme 2 October 1916
England December 1916 to March 1919
Invalided out 10 March 1919

RIXON FREDERICK
Roundwell
Married
Royal Navy
First Officer Light Vessel, Calcutta, Mombassa
Second Lieutenant 29 March 1918
Labour Battalion, Indian Army

RIXON WILLIAM
Roundwell
Married
1902 Royal Garrison Artillery

ROGERS WILLIAM ROBERT
Friar's Place
Service Number M2/120817 Lance Corporal
14th Military Ambulance, Mechanical Transport, Army Service Corps

ROSE ROBERT RICHARD †
Church Cottages, Ware Street
Single
Parents Sarah Rose and the late Robert Rose
23 February 1916 7th (Service) Battalion, The Queen's Own (Royal West Kent Regiment)
Service Number G/12307 Private
France July 1916
Died 30 September 1916, aged 19
Buried in grave X H 15, Serre Road Cemetery, Number 2, Somme, France

Robert was employed by Mr and Mrs Tasker at Danefield and then at Mr Bradley's farm, Roseacre.

A transcript of the report from the Kent Messenger, 18 November 1916:

Photograph courtesy of Kent Messenger group

Pte. R. R. Rose (Bearsted)
Royal West Kent Regiment

KILLED IN ACTION

Pte. Robert R. Rose, Royal West Kent Regiment, was killed in action, September 30th, 1916, aged 19. He joined up February 23rd 1916 and went to the Front July last. Before enlisting, he worked for Mr Bradley, Rose Acre Farm, Bearsted. His widowed mother and sisters live at Church Cottages, Ware Street, Thurnham and he has an elder brother serving in the Army Veterinary Corps.

ROSE ------
Church Cottages, Ware Street
Single
Parents Sarah Rose and the late Robert Rose
Royal Army Veterinary Corps

ROWLAND ALFRED WILLIAM
The Green
Service Number 24345 Lance Corporal
2nd Army Signal Company, Royal Engineers

ROWLAND REGINALD
The Green
Single

ROWLAND THOMAS
The Green
Single
April 1914 1st Kent Cyclist Battalion
February 1917 Alexandra, Princess of Wales's Own (Yorkshire Regiment)
June 1917 Prince Albert's (Somerset Light Infantry)
September 1917 2nd Garrison Battalion, Northumberland Fusiliers Bugler
Service Number 53684 Private
India February 1916 to September 1917
Mesopotamia September 1917 to March 1919
Demobilised 14 March 1919

ROWLAND WILLIAM
The Bakery, The Green
Single
May 1913 2nd Signal Company, Royal Engineers
Posted overseas August 1914
Lance Corporal
Demobilised 12 April 1919

A transcript of the report from the Kent Messenger, 5 December 1914

Photograph courtesy of Kent Messenger group

Pte. A. W. Rowlands, R.E.

Pte. A.W. Rowlands, Second Signal Company, R.E., is recuperating at the Royal Infirmary, Glasgow, after having been wounded at the front. A former resident of Maidstone, he is a son of Mr W. Rowland, now of the Bearsted Green Bakery, and will be remembered as an old member of the Kent Cyclists' Brigade, and of the Maidstone Swimming Club. He has kept up his natatory *(swimming)* practices while with the Army, and was last season, a member of the team which was at the head of the Inter-Unit League at Aldershot.

In a letter home Pte. Rowlands writes:- "Would you believe it. I landed in England on the 21st, and got sent to Scotland to a big hospital in Glasgow, where we are living like lords, and I am looking well on it. My head and knees are going on very well, and it will not be long before I am out of it. Altogether this makes the seventh hospital I've been in, and had my name taken about a thousand times. I expect next time I have it taken it will be for Bearsted. Roll on! I have got a holiday to come, and may be lucky enough to get it for Christmas. You talk about doing it in style. You ought to have seen three of us going through Glasgow to the hospital in an open private motor car! Swank wasn't in it – kiddies cheering and the men raising their hats.

Where I got wounded was about the hottest place I have ever been in. It's about four miles the other side of Ypres; the most forward point of our line at the time. When I got hit in the head a bombardier was with me, and he lost his head and soon as he was hit first time, and tried to run away, and it made a terrible mess of him. I bobbed down and kept there until the storm was over. When I looked up, I saw a flame, or it looked like one! I made a dash for it, and was going to run wide, as I thought, to get out of the road, and came in contact with another one. It made a clean dive and dropped about ten yards behind me. I was beginning to think I had got to go. It gives you a lovely feeling, but I think I have nearly got it off my nerves now. I will tell you more when I get home."

RUCK GEORGE HENRY
Friningham Farm
Service Number 45568
Suffolk Regiment

RUSSELL JOHN HENRY
The Street
Married
Horse Transport, Army Service Corps
Service Number 143227 Driver

SAGE BERTIE
South Budds Farm
General Base Depot, Royal Engineers
Service Number 163100 Driver

SAGE JOHN WILLIAM †
9th (Service) Battalion, Royal Sussex Regiment
Service Number SD/5681 Private
Died 31 August 1916
Commemorated Pier and Face 7C, Thiepval Memorial, Somme, France

SEAGER LEWIS
Ware Street
Royal Navy
Service Number 161507 Petty Officer
H M S Actaeon

SEARS GEORGE THOMAS
Married
1907 Royal Navy H M S Natal
Service Number 311686 Petty Officer Stoker
Died 30 December 1915
Commemorated 11, Chatham Naval Memorial

The parish magazine[2] reported George's loss in February 1916, commenting that he had married in February 1915 and that his daughter was born four days after his death.

SELVES ARTHUR JOHN
Roseacre
Married
2 January 1917 Labour Battalion, Royal Engineers
Service Number 504568 Sapper
Posted overseas 12 February 1917
also Minesweeping and Inland Water Transport
Demobilised 3 May 1919

SENT ARTHUR
Sutton Street
Single
25 October 1915 3/1st Home Counties Divisional Train, Army Service Corps
transferred 799th Company, Army Service Corps 29 October 1917
Service Number 211199 Driver
Posted overseas 19 August 1916
Salonika August 1916 to March 1919
Dorian and Vardar Front April 1917, August to September 1918
Demobilised 13 April 1919

SHARP STUART FORBES
Woodside
Major Seaforth Highlanders (Ross-shire Buffs, The Duke of Albany's)

SHERWOOD PERCY DOUGLAS
Shaw's Cottages
Married
Hampshire Cycling Corps
later 24th (County of London) Battalion, London Regiment (The Queen's), Territorial Force
Service Number 295285

SHORTER HAROLD WILLIAM
Shaw's Cottages
Single
8 August 1909 5th (Princess Charlotte of Wales's) Dragoon Guards
later City of London Yeomanry (Rough Riders)
Service Number D 3547 Private
France and Belgium August 1914 to March 1917
Mons, wounded at Charleroi
Egypt, Palestine March 1917 to June 1918
France June 1918
King's Corporal

This detail, shown below, is part of a beautiful embroidered cotton lawn handkerchief. It is an example of many small souvenirs that were sent to wives and girlfriends from serving members in the armed forces. They were known as 'Sweetheart Handkerchiefs'. Handkerchiefs with printed designs upon them were also available.

Photograph courtesy of Malcolm Kersey

SIMMONDS FREDERICK
Bearsted Spot
Single
Volunteer Training Corps later 2nd Volunteer Brigade, Royal West Kent

SIMPSON THOMAS †
1st Battalion, The Buffs (East Kent Regiment)
Service Number G/495 Corporal
Died 15 September 1916
Buried in grave XIII B 7, Guillemont Road Cemetery, Guillemont, Somme, France

SLENDER THOMAS GEORGE †
Roundwell
Single
Parents Thomas and Louisa Lucy Slender of Roundwell
November 1914 24th Signal Company, Royal Engineers
Service Number 60010 Driver
France September 1915 to February 1916
Died 12 February 1916, aged 32
Buried in grave I E 28, Poperinghe New Military Cemetery, Poperinghe, West Vlaanderen, Belgium

A transcript of the report from the Kent Messenger, 1 April 1916:

Photograph courtesy of Kent Messenger group

Driver Slender (Bearsted)
24th Signalling Co., R.E., 13th Signal Co., R.E.

KILLED IN ACTION BY HOSTILE AIRCRAFT

Mr and Mrs Slender, of Round Well, Bearsted, have received the sad news from his Captain (and the War Office) that their eldest son, Thomas George Slender, was killed on February 12th 1916 in France by a bomb from an enemy aeroplane. The Captain, in the course of a sympathetic letter said the deceased would be greatly missed by all his regiment – he was so well liked by all who knew him. The burial took place in a cemetery in France. Driver Slender enlisted in November 1914, and set sail for France in September 1915. He was 32 years of age and greatly respected, and much sympathy is felt with Mr and Mrs Slender and family in their sorrow.

A public notice which appeared in Kent Messenger, 13 February 1915:

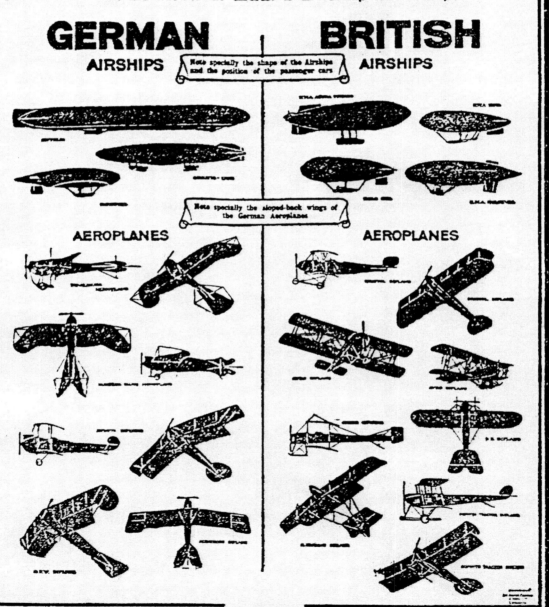

Reproduced courtesy of Kent Messenger group

SMITH ALBERT

Parsonage Farm
Married
Royal Navy 12 March 1896
Royal Fleet Reserve Royal Navy 1911 to 1914
Rejoined 2 August 1914
Leading Seaman H M S Campania
Petty Officer with North Sea Fleet 1914 to 1918
Cuxhaven Raid 25 December 1914, Destroyer Action 1 September 1917
Invalided out 19 January 1918

SMITH EDWARD JOHN

Colegate's Cottages
Single
21 October 1915 Royal Navy Division
Service Number 3547 Able Seaman
transferred Royal Naval Volunteer Reserve November 1915
Naval Air Defences Dover February 1916 to July 1918
H M S Attention II
H M S Excellent July to November 1918
H M S Vestal November 1918 to January 1919
Demobilised 20 January 1919

SMITH FRANK

Colegate's Cottages
Single
Palestine

STAPLEY WILLIAM

Roseacre
Single
Volunteer Training Corps later 2nd Volunteer Brigade, Royal West Kent

This embroidered souvenir postcard is undated, but was sent after the United States of America had entered the war, as the American flag is shown flying with those of the Allies. America declared war on Germany in 1917:

Reproduced courtesy of Brenda Iacovides

STEMP GEORGE
White Horse
Married
23 October 1916 Mechanical Transport, Army Service Corps
Posted overseas 20 October 1916 France

STERN LEOPOLD GRAHAME *†
Barty
Single
Parents L I and Lilias M Stern of Red Oaks, Henfield, Sussex
October 1917 99th Squadron, Royal Flying Corps Cadet
Second Lieutenant
France, Germany
Killed in Air Action 26 September 1918, aged 18
Buried in grave Plot 379, Chambieres French National Cemetery Metz, Moselle, France

Leopold was the pilot of De Havilland DH9 Bomber D5573, from 99 Squadron, Independent Force, Royal Air Force. He was accompanied by his Observer/Gunner Lieutenant Frederick Oliver Cook. On 26 September 1918, the squadron undertook bombing raids, supporting French and American forces around Verdun. Leopold's aircraft was re-routed from railway targets at Thionille. His aircraft was one of six that were attacked by thirty to forty enemy aircraft over Metz-Sablon around 5.10pm. Leopold's aircraft was shot down and both of the occupants were killed.[3] Parachutes were not issued to pilots and aircrew in order to discourage cowardice.

SWIFT EDGAR E †
Ware Street
Single
8th (Service) Battalion, King's (Shropshire Light Infantry)
Service Number 16897
Died 17 January 1918
Buried in grave V E 17, Doiran Military Cemetery, Greece

Edgar is buried next to Frank White who died the following day.
See entry for Frank White for further details

SWIFT STEPHEN
Egypt Cottages
Married
14 February 1916 Army Service Corps
Service Number 126514 Private
31st Squadron Remounts
France

TANNER ERNEST
Chapel Lane
Service Number 48798 Private
1st Battalion, Prince of Wales's (North Staffordshire Regiment)

TAYLOR ELGAR GEORGE
Triangle Cottages
Married
10 December 1914 61st Company, Mechanical Transport, Army Service Corps attached to 2nd Division
Posted overseas 16 December 1914

TAYLOR ERNEST GEORGE
Ware Street
Service Number 021774 Private
Mechanical Transport, Army Service Corps

TAYLOR GEORGE *
Mount Cottages
Single
Parents George and Alice Mary Taylor of Danefield Cottage
18 January 1915 13th Signal Company, Royal Engineers
Service Number 60574
Posted overseas 26 June 1915
Gallipoli June to August 1915
Cape Helles, Anzac
Killed in Action 29 August 1915, aged 19
Commemorated Panels 23-25 or 325-328, Helles Memorial, Turkey

George was born in Meopham and enlisted at Chatham. He was the brother of Edward Taylor who later ran the village newsagents in Bearsted. His father was a verger and sexton at Holy Cross church, Bearsted.

Photograph courtesy of Kent Messenger group

60574 Driv. G. Taylor (Bearsted)
13th Signal Co., R.E.

KILLED IN ACTION AT GALLIPOLI

Driver G. E. Taylor, R.E., was the son of Mr and Mrs George Taylor, of Bearsted, and his death came as a surprise to his friends. A driver in the 13th Signal Company, he was killed in the action of August 29th at Gallipoli, but notification was not received by his parents until late in September. Meanwhile, several letters which he had written had arrived, and a postcard dated August 28th, the day before his death, saying that he was all right. The news of his untimely end therefore was quite unexpected.

Joining up on January 18th, he went though his training and set out for the Dardanelles on June 26th. He had consequently landed less than two months when he was cut off, within a few weeks of his 20th birthday (which would have been on October 6th). Every sympathy has been evinced towards the bereaved parents by friends and acquaintances near and far, for the deceased was a very popular young fellow, esteemed for his bright and buoyant manner.

Mr and Mrs Taylor and family wish to sincerely acknowledge the many marks of sympathy shown towards them in their sorrow. They would also be most grateful if any member of the 13th Signal Company who might be able to give any particulars of their son's death would communicate with them at Mount Cottages, Bearsted.

TAYLOR LOUIS
White Horse
Single
7 July 1908 19th (Queen Alexandra's Own Royal) Hussars
Posted overseas 21 August 1914
France and Belgium 1914 to 1918
Germany 1919
Demobilised 29 April 1919

TAYLOR PERCY WALTER
White Horse
Married
17 February 1915 Mechanical Transport, Army Service Corps attached 25th Field Ambulance
Posted overseas 10 March 1915
France and Belgium 1915 to 1919
Demobilised 17 February 1919

Percy married Miss Wingate on 23 January 1916. It was reported in the parish magazine in February[4] that Percy came home from the Front on Thursday and they were married by special licence on Sunday. The following Friday, he returned to the Front.

This postcard is an excellent example of the many elaborately embroidered cards that were sent from the troops serving at the Front. It would be good to think that Percy found time to send a similar card to his new wife.

Reproduced courtesy of Brenda Iacovides

TAYLOR STEPHEN
White Horse
Single
1 May 1916 Mechanical Transport, Army Service Corps attached 25th Field Ambulance
Posted overseas 17 May 1916
France and Belgium 1916
Prisoner of War May to November 1918
Demobilised 26 August 1919

A transcript of the report from the Kent Messenger, 20 July 1918

Information Wanted

Photograph courtesy of Kent Messenger group

Stephen Taylor (Bearsted)
Motor Field Ambulance

MISSING

Mr and Mrs W. W. Taylor of the White Horse, Bearsted, have been officially notified by the War Office that their son, Stephen Taylor, 25th Motor Field Ambulance, 8th Division, has been missing since May 27th 1918. He joined up on May 6th 1916 (having previously been chauffeur to Lieut. Colonel A. Wood-Martyn) and went over to France on the 15th. He was home on his last leave in October 1917. Three other sons and a son in law of Mr and Mrs Taylor are all serving in France and it was Stephen's brother Percy, (who himself had a 'narrow escape' from being captured), who first reported home that he believed Stephen to have been taken prisoner. If anyone can furnish any information respecting him, the family would be deeply grateful.

TAYLOR WALTER
Ware Street
Service Number M2 143131 Private
46th Divisional Motor Transport Company, Army Service Corps

TAYLOR WILLIAM LOUIS
White Horse
Married
9 November 1910 9th (Queen's Royal) Lancers
transferred Machine Gun Corps (Cavalry) May 1917 later 19th (Queen Alexandra's Own Royal) Hussars
Service Number 2677 Private
Posted overseas 15 August 1914
France August 1914 to January 1917, March 1917 to February 1919
Ireland January to March 1917
Mons, Marne, Aisne, Ypres, Cambrai, Somme
Wounded
Demobilised 13 March 1919

TESTER CHARLES
Forge Cottages
Married
Volunteer Training Corps later 2nd Volunteer Brigade, Royal West Kent

Charles was a blacksmith and farrier. He served for some of the war with the 5th (Reserve) Battalion, King's Royal Rifle Corps, Transport Division. This photograph shows him in the middle of the back row.

Photograph courtesy of John Mills

THOMPSON WILFRED ARTHUR
Tollgate
Married
September 1895 Royal Navy
Lieutenant-Commander H M S Glasgow
Commander H M S Roberts, H M S Martin
Falkland Island Battle

TOMSETT WILLIAM THOMAS
1 Fancy Row
Service Number 171563 Private
309th (Home Service) Works Company, Army Service Corps

TOLHURST FRIEND
Crisfield Cottage
Married
5 July 1918 Army Service Corps attached 178th Tunnelling Company, Royal Engineers
Posted overseas 5 November 1918
France November 1918 to June 1919
Demobilised 18 June 1919

TOWN STEPHEN
The Street
Single
31 October 1914 Royal Army Medical Corps, Territorial Force
Service Number 49370 Private
Posted overseas 16 August 1916
Salonika August 1916 to December 1918
Struma Valley
Demobilised 9 January 1919

TOWN THOMAS CHARLES

The Street
Single
April 1915 Army Service Corps
Lance-corporal
Posted overseas July 1915

TREE ALFRED EDWARD

The Green
Single
July 1918 51st Graduated Battalion, Queen's (Royal West Surrey Regiment)

TROWELL WILLIAM HENRY

Detling Hill
Royal Navy
Service Number 2842536 Chief Stoker
H M S Bacchante

TUDD THOMAS

Roseacre
Inland Waterways & Docks, Royal Engineers
Service Number 333551

TURVEY ARTHUR

Ware Street
1st Battalion, Grenadier Guards
Service Number 24857 Private

WALKER ARTHUR FRANCIS GREGORY

Tollgate
Married
1 January 1915 8th Battalion, East Lancashire Regiment
Posted overseas 24 July 1915 France
Staff Captain 112th Infantry Brigade
General Staff Officer 3rd Grade, 33rd Division March 1917
Wounded at Ypres 1917
Brigade Major 1918
11th Cyclist Brigade 1919
Deputy Assistant Adjutant General Eastern Command
Arras 1917, Ypres
Military Cross (London Gazette, January 1918)
Mentioned in despatches
Demobilised 31 March 1919

WALKLING ALBERT

3 Egypt Place
Married
1 June 1915 21st (County of London) Battalion, London Regiment (1st Surrey Rifles), Territorial Force
Service Number 64026 Private
Posted overseas 28 December 1916 France
Attached to Balloon Section, Royal Air Force Italy 1 November 1917
France 4 February 1918
Ypres, Messines, Passchendaele, Merville
Demobilised April 1919

WALKLING ALFRED THOMAS
The Street
Service Number T4 211223 Wheeler Corporal
Base Depot, Army Service Corps

WALKLING FRANK CHARLES
South View
Single
7 October 1915 Suffolk Regiment later 8th (Service) Battalion, King's Own Yorkshire Light Infantry
Service Number 37610 Private

WALKLING THOMAS
South View
Single
October 1915 Army Service Corps
Corporal
France
Demobilised 4 June 1919

WALTER ALFRED JESSE
Oliver's Row
Married
July 1915 Mechanical Transport, Army Service Corps
Lance-corporal
Posted overseas August 1915 France
Somme, Messines, Cambrai, Lille, Tournai
Demobilised 29 May 1919

WATCHAM ALFRED JOHN
Golf House
Married
27 October 1916 Essex Regiment
Invalided out 27 February 1918

WATCHAM FREDERICK
Church Cottage
Married
15 October 1915 Royal Navy Division, Anti Aircraft Defences Dover
Royal Naval Volunteer Reserve 1916 Able Seaman
Defensively Armed Merchant Ships
Seaman on Steam Ship Corinthian wrecked off Nova Scotia December 1918
H M S Victory 1919

WATKINS A
Croix-de-Guerre

WATKINS LESLIE †
Ware Street
Single
Parents Mr and Mrs Alfred Watkins of Ware Street
7th (Service) Battalion, The Queen's Own (Royal West Kent Regiment)
Service Number G/20607 Private
Posted as missing, presumed killed, 21 March 1918
Commemorated Panel 58 and 59, Pozieres Memorial, Albert, Somme

A transcript of the report from the Kent Messenger, 1 June 1918

Photograph courtesy of the Kent Messenger group

Pte. Leslie Watkins (Bearsted)
Royal West Kent Regiment

MISSING

Leslie Watkins, aged 19, is the youngest of the six fighting sons of Mr and Mrs Alfred Watkins of Station Hill, Bearsted. He was, on attaining the age of 18, called up from his employment at the Japanese Embassy, London, when the youngest boy of the family, Albert, took his position. Leslie went out to France early in the present year with a draft of the Royal West Kents, and has been missing since the 21st March. Letters and cigarettes sent to him since have been returned intact. In reply to inquiries by his parents, the War Office, his commanding officer, and the chaplain, all say they can only report him as missing. Any information with regard to him would be most gratefully received by his parents at the above address.

WATKINS PERCY ARTHUR CUMMINGS
Ware Street
Single
Parents Mr and Mrs Alfred Watkins of Ware Street
Army Service Corps

This undated photograph shows an unknown member of the Watkins family in the uniform of The Buffs (East Kent Regiment):

Photograph courtesy of Jean Jones

WATTS HENRY HERBERT ERIC
Holmleigh
Single
25 January 1915 3/1st City of London Field Ambulance
later 2/1st Field Ambulance, Royal Army Medical Corps
Service Number 508368 Private
Posted overseas 21 February 1916
France and Belgium February 1916 to March 1919
Somme, First, Second, Third Battle of Arras, Third Battle of Ypres, Bullecourt, Cambrai, Mons 1918
Demobilised 20 March 1919

WELLARD CHARLES WILLIAM *
South View
Single
Parents Mr C E and Mrs L Wellard, South View
March 1918 1/8th Battalion, Duke of Cambridge's Own (Middlesex Regiment), Territorial Force
Service Number 54745 Lance Corporal
Posted overseas August 1918 France
Killed on Active Service 12 October 1918, Aged 18
Buried in grave ID 12, Cagnicourt British Cemetery, Pas de Calais, France

Charles was born at Frinsted and enlisted in Maidstone. His father was village Police Constable in Bearsted for a time.

A transcript of the report from the Kent Messenger, 2 November 1918:

Photograph courtesy of Kent Messenger group

Lce-Cpl. C. W. Wellard (Bearsted)
Middlesex Regiment

KILLED IN ACTION

Lce-Corpl. C. W. Wellard, elder son of P.C. and Mrs Wellard of Bearsted, was killed in action on October 12th. He was 18 years of age, an old Volunteer, and was formerly employed at the Kent County Council Offices at Maidstone.

WHITE ALFRED
Ware Street
Service Number 10798 Lance Corporal
11th (Service) Battalion, King's Royal Rifle Corps

WHITE CARIE
Honor Oak
Single
June 1917 Women's Army Auxiliary Corps
Demobilised 15 April 1919

WHITE ERNEST ALBERT †
2 Chapel Lane, Ware Street
Married
Wife Agnes Elizabeth White
Children Agnes and Ernest
Parents Frederick Horace and Emma Jane White of Ware Street, Thurnham
2nd Battalion, Royal Fusiliers (City of London Regiment)
Service Number 46714 Private
Died 19 August 1918, aged 26
Buried in grave II E 60, Rue-Petillon Military Cemetery, Fleurbaix, Pas de Calais, France

Ernest was killed before his second child was born.

WHITE FRANK †
Ware Street
Single
Parents Clara White and the late Albert White
1915 8th (Service) Battalion, King's (Shropshire Light Infantry)
Service Number 16898 Private
Died 18 January 1918, aged 26
Buried in grave V E 18, Doiran Military Cemetery, Greece

A partial transcript of the report from the Kent Messenger, 23 February 1918:

Picture courtesy of Kent Messenger group

Pte. Frank White (Thurnham)
Shropshire Light Infantry

Mrs C White, of Ware Street, Thurnham, has received the sad news of the death of her son, Private Frank White, of the Shropshire Light Infantry, at the front at Salonika. He was badly wounded by a shell on January 18th and only lived about two and a half hours after. He had been in the Army three years, of which he was in Salonika two years and four months. Before he joined he was under gardener for Mr W. R. Prosser, Ardenlee, Sittingbourne Road, Maidstone for four years and afterwards for Sir Reginald MacLeod, K.C.B., at Vinters Park.

Frank White was much esteemed during his career as a soldier as well as in private life as the sympathetic letters to his widowed mother from his Colonel and his Captain amply testify. Mrs White, whose husband died at Netley Hospital during the Boer War, has also had several letters from comrades of her son, Frank, speaking most highly of him and deploring his death. It appears that the same shell that killed him also killed Edgar Swift, the son of a neighbour in Ware Street. They had been schoolmates together, worked together, joined up and went out together, fought side by side, died together and were buried together. Frank White was 26 years of age. At home he had always taken a keen interest in cricket, football and other sports and was most highly esteemed.

WHITE FREDERICK
2 West View
Married
8 May 1916 Royal Field Artillery
Service Number 145737 Gunner
13th Division GAAS
Posted overseas 13 September 1916
Mesopotamia October 1916 to August 1918
Recapture of Kut, Baghdad to Kirkuk
Demobilised 13 February 1919

WHITE FREDERICK HORACE
Ware Street
1st Battalion, The Queen's Own (Royal West Kent Regiment)
Service Number 265289 Lance Corporal

WHITE PERCY GEORGE
Honor Oak
Single
10 November 1915 2nd County of London Yeomanry (Westminster Dragoons)
1916 Royal Field Artillery Gunner
Service Number 945053
Posted overseas 6 February 1917
France February 1917 to September 1918
Arras 1917, March Retreat, Marne, Somme 1918
Wounded
Demobilised 10 January 1919

WHITE P H
14 St Peter's Street, Maidstone
Married
2/4th Battalion, The Queen's Own (Royal West Kent Regiment), Territorial Force
Service Number TF/3582
Posted overseas 19 July 1915
Died 21 September 1915 of enteric fever
Buried in grave B XIII 5, Pieta Military Cemetery, Malta

A transcript of the report from the Kent Messenger, 26 February 1916:

Photograph courtesy of Kent Messenger group

Pte P. H. White (Maidstone)
Royal West Kent Regiment

DIED AT MALTA

Pte. P. H. White of the 2/4th Royal West Kent Regiment, which left Bedford July 19th for the Dardanelles, died of enteric fever at Malta September 21st 1915. He was born at Bearsted, and before enlisting was in the gardens of Mr R. J. Balston, for 12 years. He leaves a widow and six children (the eldest 12 years of age) at 14 St Peter's Street, Maidstone, to mourn their loss.

WHITE STANLEY THOMAS
Honor Oak
Single
20 January 1915 Royal Naval Air Service and Royal Air Force
Chief Mechanic
Service Number 203192 Petty Officer
France August 1916 to May 1917
Italy May 1917 to February 1918
Dunkirk, Piave
Demobilised February 1919

WHITE WALTER FREDERICK
Honor Oak
Single
14 August 1914 Kent Cyclist Battalion
Posted overseas November 1914
Second Lieutenant later Lieutenant The Queen's Own (Royal West Kent Regiment)

WHITE WALTER VICTOR
Ware Street
1st Battalion, The Queen's Own (Royal West Kent Regiment)
Service Number 265290 Lance Corporal

WHITEHEAD WILLIAM HINGESTON

The Mount
Married
1915 Lieutenant The Queen's Own (Royal West Kent Regiment) Reserve Training
Retired 1918

William was Chairman of Bearsted Parish Council 1909-1949

WICKENS GEORGE ARTHUR

The Street
Married
14 October 1914 West Kent Yeomanry (Queen's Own)
Service Number 492063 Private
later 684th Agricultural Company, Army Service Corps
France
Demobilised 5 March 1919

WILKINSON ARTHUR *

Mote Villas
Single
Service Number 4846
2nd also 9th (Service) Battalion, Royal Fusiliers (City of London Regiment)
France
Missing, presumed killed 4 August 1916
Commemorated IV J 36, Pozieres British Cemetery Ovillers la Boisselle, Somme, France
Bearsted war memorial date is 4 August 1918

Arthur was born at Mote Hall Villas. He resided and enlisted in East Ham. His father Charles was an Old Scholar and Manager of Bearsted School. Charles was a builder and undertaker.

WILKINSON CHARLES

Mote Villas
Single
2 November 1915 Royal Engineers
Service Number 140150 Sapper
Posted overseas 31 July 1916
Mesopotamia August 1916 to July 1918
Persia June to December 1918
Caucasus December 1918 to April 1919
Recapture of Kut, Capture of Baghdad, Dunsterville Expedition in Persia.
Demobilised 24 June 1919

WILKINSON FREDERICK *

Mote Villas
Single
11th (Service) (Cambridgeshire) Battalion, Suffolk Regiment
Service Number 41446
Lance corporal
France February 1917 Training Reserve Battalion
Killed in Action 22 March 1918
Commemorated Bay 4, Arras Memorial, Pas de Calais, France

WILKINSON WILFRED

Mote Villas
Single
2 November 1915 Royal Engineers Driver
Service Number 141023
Demobilised 8 January 1919

Wilfred was born in 1891. He married Florence Sent at Holy Cross church, Bearsted in October 1922.

WILKINSON WILLIAM JESSE

The Street
Married
26 October 1916 King's Royal Rifle Corps
Service Number 31857
Demobilised 22 February 1919

WISDOM ALBERT JOHN *

Acacia Villas, Willington Road
Single
Parents Solomon and Elizabeth Wisdom, Acacia Villas, Willington Road
May 1915 Royal Navy
Service Number London Z/2197 Able Seaman
H M S Nottingham and H M S Laurentic
Lost at Sea from H M S Laurentic in a mine explosion off the Irish coast, 25 January 1917 aged 19
Commemorated Chatham Naval Memorial and on the war memorial plaque at St Nicholas church, Otham.

WISDOM GEORGE SOLOMON

Acacia Villas, Willington Road
Single
Parents Solomon and Elizabeth Wisdom, Acacia Villas, Willington Road
1906 Royal Navy
Service Number 236381 Leading Seaman
H M S Apollo, H M S Bat

WISDOM SOLOMON

4 Willington Road
Married
23 March 1915 5th Battalion, The Queen's Own (Royal West Kent Regiment), Territorial Force
later 162nd Company, Royal Defence Corps
Service Number 1801 Private
Demobilised 11 March 1919

WISDOM WILLIAM HENRY

Acacia Villas, Willington Road
Single
1913 Royal Navy
Service Number K 19272 Stoker 1st Class
H M S Africa

Walter Fremlin, who lived at Milgate Park, decided to commemorate the end of the war. He was a brewer and hop grower. He and his wife had no children, but they had been immensely saddened by the number of casualties in the war and the effect of the losses upon local families. He therefore gave each of his employee's children a War Savings Certificate, worth fifteen shillings and sixpence. This certificate and compliments card was given to Eileen Blandford:

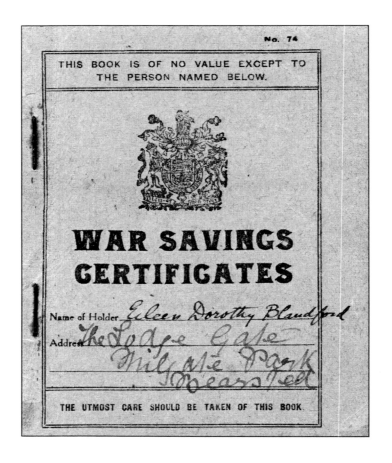

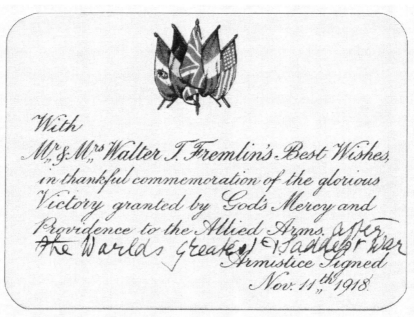

Reproduced courtesy of Jenni Hudson

Once the Armistice was signed, it did not take long for local companies to highlight that their goods were suitable for peacetime, as this advertisement shows which appeared in Kent Messenger, 25 January 1919:

DEMOBILIZATION!
From Service Dress into Civilian Clothing.
As hundreds of thousands of young men
will shortly be leaving the Colours,

GEO. H. LEAVEY & Co., Ltd.
have prepared a REALLY MAGNIFICENT STOCK of

MEN'S SUITS
:: READY FOR SERVICE ::
All at VERY MODERATE PRICES, and every Suit GUARANTEED TO
WEAR THOROUGHLY WELL.

Not a single low grade cloth will be found in this selection, and the value is excellent in comparison with today's prices.

Every size in stock from 32 to 42 breast and 29 to 35 leg, for tall, short or normal figures. Thus 14 out of every 15 men can be fitted exactly from stock.

PRICES PER SUIT:
£2 15 0 (£3 0 0 Gov. Standard), £3 7 6, £3 15 0,
£3 19 0, £4 4 0, £4 10 0 and £4 15 0.

OVERCOATS. Gov. Standard £3 3 0, also in Double or Single Breast at
£3 10 0, £3 19 0, £4 4 0, £4 10 0 & £5 5 0

High Street and Mill Street, Maidstone.

Reproduced courtesy of Kent Messenger group

Memories of the First World War

There seem to be very few details about every day life in Bearsted and Thurnham during the First World War that have been written down. Mr Thomas Gilbert's memories were recorded when he was around ninety years old, by the now disbanded Thurnham History Group. Miss Grace Dibble's memories were published in 1989.[1] Mr Cornford also published a booklet about Detling in 1980[2] which included some information about Thurnham.

The Gilbert family moved to Ware Street in the early 1900s. Thomas was usually known as Tom. He recalled that during the first decade of the Twentieth century some men emigrated to Canada and joined the armed forces there. The rest of their families continued to live in Ware Street and regularly received money that was sent home. For many men, joining the army seemed an attractive option: in addition to the chance for adventure and a better way of life, a ready supply of food and accommodation was guaranteed.

There were two major explosions in Sheerness dockyard during the war that would have been heard over a long distance. Tom particularly recalled 27 May 1915, a detonation was heard in Ware Street and Thurnham. It was some time before it was learned that the cause was the explosion of a Canadian Pacific liner called The Princess Irene. The liner was being converted for mine laying. A large number of Sheerness dockyard workers lost their lives.[3]

There were occasions during the war when six small airships would appear over Thurnham Hill for bombing practice. A series of trenches had been dug along the top of the Downs in preparation for possible invasion. At the top of Thurnham parish was Detling aerodrome. Parts of the Medway estuary were less than four miles away from Thurnham and Stockbury, so there were at least two reasons why the area was deemed vulnerable. One air ship looked like three joined together and earned the nickname 'the three sausages' although Tom thought that the real name might have been 'blimps'. Tom used to join his friends exploring the trenches. One favourite place was a covered dugout which the troops had named 'Ginger Beer Redoubt'.

In the spring of 1916, Tom Gilbert's father was in the Army. However, the pay was very low. There was an additional separation allowance that was paid to some families but it was not very much, so money was scarce. It was decided that Tom should leave school. He was nearly thirteen when he went to work. His first wages were six shillings a week. In the absence of his father, he was regarded as the 'man of the house'. The chores he had to perform included tending the garden and allotment. Many people grew enormous amounts of vegetables to boost a small family income. Tom's experience of leaving his childhood behind to assume adult responsibilities was a common one for many boys in Thurnham and Bearsted during the war.

* * * *

Michael Perring has been able to confirm Tom's information about the trenches. The earthworks formed part of the Chatham first line of defence. They were dug by the Kent Fortress Royal Engineers and Infantrymen along the northern side of Detling Hill and the Stockbury valley.[4] The earthworks passed through the northernmost parts of Thurnham parish at Binbury and Beaux Aires. In addition to defence, they were also used for training by the 12th Battalion of the Royal Sussex Regiment. Mr Cornford recalled that when he was a boy in 1915, soldiers set up a tented camp on the Pilgrims Way, between Detling and Thurnham. A few yards behind the field gate a soldier was on guard. He wore a khaki uniform and carried an Enfield rifle. During the summer the soldiers marched up Thurnham Lane in one column, four abreast, led by a brass band. He believed that the trenches were used by the men to learn the art of trench warfare. Mrs Sybil Trowell also recalled that the soldiers even constructed a facility that could be used as an underground hospital.[5]

Although the aerodrome established in 1914 was named after Detling, much of the land was in Thurnham. The level hilltop area to the south and east of Binbury Manor was opened as an air defence landing ground with naval aviators and aircraft accommodated in tents and canvas hangars before permanent buildings were constructed.[6] Some of the plane crews were billeted in local houses.[7] The first planes at the aerodrome arrived in a convoy of Leyland lorries. Each one carried a large, rectangular wooden box. Many boys in Detling believed that each box contained all the parts needed to make one aeroplane.[8] Manoeuvres and flying exercises began around 1915. The local residents were told that the aeroplanes would practice dropping bombs and that the shock waves from exploding bombs might cause damage to buildings. It was left to the householders to decide whether or not to protect their property. In the event, there were no explosions or damage to houses, but practice bombs were dropped.[9] By 1916 Detling was used by A Flight of 50 Squadron and B Flight arrived in August 1917. The aerodrome was transferred to the Royal Flying Crops in 1917.[10] 143 Squadron was formed there in February 1918,[11] and was very active against German bombers.[12]

Another part of Thurnham was involved in defence research. Airship raids on the Humber and Thames estuaries in May 1915 highlighted the need for some sort of early warning system. Experiments with sound mirrors had taken place elsewhere in 1914, but in July 1915 further trials were started at Binbury in the north western extremity of Thurnham. However, it is not clear why Binbury was chosen. Despite the close proximity of Detling aerodrome, the aircraft used in the tests where flown in from other locations.

Professor Mather of the City and Guilds Engineering College in South Kensington, arranged for a sound mirror, approximately sixteen feet in diameter, to be cut into the chalk cliff face at Binbury Farm, then owned by Mr Murray.[13] A section of the vertical cliff face was hollowed out to an almost spherical shape that was tilted upwards and a sound collector was mounted on a pivot at the focal point. The apparatus was rather like a stethoscope whereby a person could listen to sounds detected by a trumpet shaped cone. The collector could be moved across the face of the mirror to establish where the sound was loudest. It was envisaged that the reflector could sweep up to thirty degrees of the horizon.[14] Bearings to the target could then be read from vertical and horizontal scales on the collector.[15] In the subsequent report it was claimed:

> It is extremely probable that a Zeppelin with its very large engines and gearing would be easily heard at a distance of twenty miles. We think a concrete reflector of sixteen feet diameter would be superior to one of chalk as the reflecting surface would be harder…[16]

Despite disappointing results in subsequent experiments carried out by the Army in Wiltshire, several mirrors lined with concrete were constructed around the south-east coast. These later mirrors were evidently able to successfully detect enemy aircraft as the reports were sent to a central command centre to assist defensive measures during raids in 1917 and 1918.[17]

* * * *

At the start of the war, Grace Dibble's family lived at The Poplars, Roseacre Lane. She recalled:[18]

> At home in Bearsted there had been murmurs of the possibility of war with Germany. But it was an unpleasant shock on August 4th, when I came out of the railway station in the early evening to be told by a neighbour, "It's war!" I was returning from a birthday party in the home of a school friend in Lenham, where we had enjoyed ourselves and there was no talk of war. Aged only twelve years, I could not appreciate all the incomprehensible horrors of the future.

> After the initial shock, it was soon brought home to us what it meant to the village as men enlisted, then appeared briefly in khaki before embarkation. These were young men whom we knew and many whom mother had taught in the village school. At once women were organised to do knitting and sewing, with khaki wool and materials provided. My sister and I had learned to knit father's long cycling stockings and our own stockings, so that it was easy for us to knit socks for the Forces. In the nearby Mission Room there were women cutting up materials for pyjamas or three-tailed bandages. The latter we found puzzling at first. We wound endless skeins of wool. I particularly hated knitting the very long stockings in natural greasy wool, to be worn with rubber boots. 100 garments were sent to the depot in Maidstone.

We could hear the planes flying over our area to raid London. During daytime raids, as on Chatham, we were assembled in the corridors in the Maidstone Grammar School for Girls. Once I was spending a weekend with a school friend in East Malling, when we went down into the cellar during a raid. This was the first time I had this frightening experience. Later in the war we had to go down into our own damp, cold and dark cellar during raids. One bomb did drop not far off, in Chapel Lane.

Once father organised the billeting of soldiers in Bearsted and Thurnham, on their way to France. Our house was full and our beds were given up to the troops, while we slept on the floor. We fed them in relays, with roast beef and apple pie for dinner. The men were from a brigade of the Royal Sussex Regiment, so for a long time afterwards we frequently sang "Sussex by the Sea", after we had bought a copy of the song. Some of them were in a tented camp in Detling at the foot of the North Downs. We soon learned other songs: "It's a long way to Tipperary", "Keep the Home fires burning" and "Pack up your troubles in your old Kit Bag".

Another memorable occasion was when a troop-train broke down in the cutting opposite to our house. The train stretched back as far as the road bridge. It was too heavy to cope with the incline of 1-60 up to Bearsted Station. From Maidstone there is a rise of 150 feet in the two and three-quarter miles. It was in early autumn, so we loaded up baths with Beauty of Bath apples, taking them across the road and through Mr Hodges' garden to lower down the bank to the train. We were accustomed to seeing the troop-trains crossing the bridge on their way to the coast. We used to wave to them. We hated to see these young men going overseas, especially after casualties were announced in church and printed in the parish magazine, and local newspapers.

The first death was George Taylor in Gallipoli, in August 1915. Later that year came the news of the death of our curate, Captain W. M. Benton, who had at once joined up as a fighting officer and not as a chaplain. As we would have expected, he was killed while rescuing a wounded soldier. The next year we were distressed to hear that Charles Wilkinson, Christian Message and Robert Rose had been killed in action. At sea Reggie Ball lost his life. In Ware Street the inhumanity of war was emphasised when our milkman, Harry Hodges had to return after suffering a very bad gas attack – something from which he never really recovered.

But there were cheerful occasions when we were especially proud of our men from Bearsted and Thurnham. In 1916, James Frazier was awarded the Distinguished Conduct Medal. Two years later our baker, Lance Corporal Lionel Datson was awarded the Military Medal. Showing great courage, he brought his ambulance three times through a village which was being shelled, thus enabling a dressing station to be cleared of wounded. Major Daniell was awarded the Russian Order of St. Stanislav of the 2nd Class in 1918. We were proud of Dora Harnett who had joined the Women's Army Auxiliary Corps, and was sent to France, as a driver, attached to Army Service Corps.

There were ripples of pride when Mr and Mrs Mannering received a letter from King George V, congratulating them on having five sons in the army...My father became a sergeant in the Volunteer Training Corps in Bearsted. He was proud of his khaki uniform and little cane. Men who were over thirty-eight years or unfit for active service met in a hall behind the White Horse Inn for rifle shooting on three days in the week. Then there was attendance at a camp near Canterbury for training: father conscientiously studied the special handbook.

Many people in Britain were put in touch with prisoners of war in German prisons. We adopted one in Berlin and used to send him parcels of socks and food which we could spare, in tins. Of course, there came rationing of foods. We were fortunate in that Auntie Lucy in Gloucestershire regularly sent us a pound of her farm butter in a tin. I remember how we hated maize pudding, as a substitute for rice. We also disliked the shortage of sugar. The members of the Women's Institute gained a reputation for their jams and marmalades. Near the village shops a local jam factory was initiated to use fruits from the orchards.

The daily newspapers kept us informed about events beyond Bearsted and overseas. It was a shock to many families when conscription was made compulsory in 1915. It was not easy to appreciate the great horrors in 1916 when the Zeppelins bombed London.

I shall never forget Armistice Day on November 11th, 1918. At the Maidstone Girls' Grammar School, we were all in the playground waiting for Miss Jones to return on her bicycle to hear it, if it was really true that the war had at last ended. When the joyful news was brought, we trooped into the hall and sang, "Praise my soul, the King of Heaven".

After the Armistice had been signed, King George V approved a plan to hold a Peace Day on 19 July 1919. Celebrations were held on a local basis throughout the country. Bearsted and Thurnham combined for their Peace Day events. A transcript of the report from Kent Messenger, 26 July 1919:

BEARSTED & THURNHAM

Bearsted and Thurnham, being so intermixed, joined up for their Peace Celebrations at historic Bearsted Green. Most people were awakened in the early morning by a dreamy haunting sound of universal bell ringing with which the air seemed filled, and at 7 o'clock came the sound of the joy-guns from the old Crimean cannon in Milgate Park. From the main turret of the old church floated the grand old flag. The band of the 2nd Battalion Royal West Kents under Band Sergt J Coombes, played selections of music, and there were sports of all kinds for children, women and men, many of which were sources of immense amusement, and the beauty of it was that class distinctions were dropped and all joined together in the various competitions. In the tug-of-war competition the women of Thurnham defeated Bearsted, but in the men's final tussle, Bearsted became victorious.

The school children to the number of 230, were entertained to a substantial tea in the White Horse Hall, which had been tastefully decorated and later some 204 people were similarly entertained, while coffee, tea, tobacco and other luxuries were sent to such as were unable to attend.

The fancy dress carnival was a great success in which the crowd made a picture of marvellously picturesque beauty and life. Out of so many really excellent 'get-ups' it would be almost invidious to particularise and the characters included Mr Oswald Jones with the big drum leading as Showman; Mr A Spenceley's, Peace Dove; Mrs George Stemp, Buchanan's Black-and-White; Mr H Brook, The Scarlet Pimpernel; Mr Slingsby's, Jolly Jack Tar with concertina; Mr Tom Presland, a Death or Glory Boy with bones; Miss Violet Hunt, a Jockey, and Mr Bert Baker, a Mandarin, while Mr Gus Carr as a Crossing Sweeper, might have been the Pied Piper of Hamelin the way the children followed his antics with his besom.

Then came a comic football match, and a fancy dress dance over which Mr Tom Hickmott ruled as M C and in which an outstanding feature was a little old lady in an old fashioned bonnet and Paisley shawl, who, immediately the music struck up, stood alone and pirouetted demurely. She turned out to be Miss Isabel Hawkes, an esteemed maid at Milgate Park and she certainly brought even the very aroma of the past into to the gay scene.

Then came a grand march past, headed by the amusing Bearsted Fancy Dress Band, the distribution of prizes, the magnificent firework display and the huge bonfire which could be seen for miles around.

Major McQueen had an arduous task as Chairman of the various Committees and he was assisted by Messrs W H Whitehead, Dibble and Dewhurst, Colonel and Mr H V Lushington and many others, while Mr W Prime Jones had his hands full as M C over the day's doings as a whole. Amid the throng on the Green moved Mr and Mrs Walter T Fremlin and party, the Baroness Orczy, Mr Montague Barstow, Mr Jack Barstow and friends, who took a lively interest in the gay festivities. Mrs H Brook and Mrs A Spence were mainly responsible, with much willing help at the tea.

Over £50 had been subscribed voluntarily for the celebrations and Mr Walter Fremlin defrayed the cost of the fireworks, etc., which were under the direction of Mr Stanley Johnson. Everyone voted the Celebration an unqualified success.

Reproduced courtesy of Kent Messenger group

Welcome Home: First World War

After the war had ended, a series of dinners was held at the White Horse, Bearsted to welcome back returned members of the armed forces. A transcript of the report from the Kent Messenger, June 1919:

BEARSTED AND THE WAR

Entertaining the Returned Heroes

'Bearsted bares her blushing honours thick upon her with a modesty well becoming her present prestige in the annals of England's glory' as some most interesting details that came out on Thursday evening go to show. The occasion was a friendly smoking concert got up amongst 'the boys' themselves who have been 'demobbed' and held at the White Horse Assembly Rooms which had been tastefully decorated for the occasion. Mr Thomas Presland, R.N., occupied the chair, and the guests, with a few invited friends numbered about 150, the proceedings being characterised throughout with much patriotic enthusiasm and gusto. Mr Presland thanked the people of Bearsted very heartily for their thoughtful kindliness in sending parcels and comforts to the sick, wounded, prisoners and others, and stated that the number of men from the village who joined up was approximately 100, killed or died of wounds 27, wounded 40 per cent.

The honours gained had been as follows:- James Fraser D.C.M., Lionel Datson and Sergeant Sid Attwood the M.M., Chief Petty Officer Dick Goodhew, the Croix-de-Guerre and the Italian Order, A Watkins, the Croix-de-Guerre, P Holmes, the Russian Order, and Harold Shorter had been made a King's Corporal.

The village had good cause to be very proud of such a fine record, and it was a great pleasure to him to present, on behalf of those of his comrades, a handsome watch with suitable inscription: 'to James Frazer in recognition of the noble exploit in the field that had gained him the D.C.M.'. Mr James Frazer, in acknowledging the gift, said he had certainly gained the D.C.M., but they had all been fighting alike for the old folks at home, and had each been doing his bit.

His joy was somewhat marred by the sorrowful reflection, that during the ten years he had been on service, he had lost both father and mother, who would today have felt so proud to see him honoured by his King and fellow villagers alike. His emotion would not permit him to say more than to thank them all (applause).

Mr John Baker proposed the toast of 'absent friends', among whom he included those who were unable to be present for various reasons, those who are still doing their bit, and those sacred ones who had fallen and made the great sacrifice. The company drank the toast standing in silence.

Mr E G Taylor, of Thurnham, proposed the toast of 'The good friends of the village, who did so much for us in the war', in the way of parcels of necessaries and comforts, of which good work, he said, the White Horse appeared to have been the grand headquarters. (applause). He referred with regret to the death of Mr W W Taylor, and expressed sympathy with Mrs Taylor and the bereaved family. Mr George White responded.

Mr Doughty, Maidstone Secretary of the Comrades of the Great War, spoke briefly on the aims and objects of his society. Mr B Pearce of Maidstone, presided at the piano, and among those who contributed to the harmony of the evening were Messrs Harry Pearce, Tom Walkling, John Watson, Doughty, Harry Apps, A Selves, F Pratt, W Frazer, James Frazer (by special request 'Neuve Chapelle'), Albert Baker, Tom Presland, Harold Shorter, C Peck, Ernest Farewell, E G Taylor and others.

Reproduced courtesy of Kent Messenger group

Second World War: 1939 to 1945

A transcript of the main reports from the Daily Mirror, 4 September 1939:

BRITAIN'S FIRST DAY OF WAR; CHURCHILL IS NEW NAVY CHIEF

BRITAIN AND GERMANY HAVE BEEN AT WAR SINCE ELEVEN O'CLOCK YESTERDAY MORNING. FRANCE AND GERMANY HAVE BEEN AT WAR SINCE YESTERDAY AT 5pm

A British War Cabinet of nine members was set up last night. Mr Winston Churchill, who was First Lord of the Admiralty when Britain last went to war, returns to that post.

Full list of the War Cabinet is:-

PRIME MINISTER	**Mr Neville Chamberlain**
CHANCELLOR OF THE EXCHEQUER	**Sir John Simon**
FOREIGN SECRETARY	**Viscount Halifax**
DEFENCE MINISTER	**Lord Chatfield**
FIRST LORD	**Mr Winston Churchill**
SECRETARY FOR WAR	**Mr Leslie Hore-Belisha**
SECRETARY FOR AIR	**Sir Kingsley Wood**
LORD PRIVY SEAL	**Sir Samuel Hoare**
MINISTER WITHOUT PORTFOLIO	**Lord Hankey**

There are other Ministerial changes. Mr Eden becomes Dominions Secretary, Sir Thomas Inskip goes to the House of Lords as Lord Chancellor, Lord Stanhope, ex-First Lord, becomes Lord President of the Council, Sir John Anderson is the Home Secretary and Minister of Home Security – a new title. None of these is in the Cabinet, which is restricted to the Big Nine. These are the men who will be responsible for carrying on the war. But Mr Eden is to have special access to the Cabinet. The Liberal Party explained last night that although Sir Archibald Sinclair had been offered a ministerial post, the Party had decided at this moment not to enter the Government.

Petrol Will Be Rationed

The first meeting of the new war Cabinet took place last night. Mr Churchill was the first to leave and the crowd broke into a cheer as he walked out. Mr Hore-Belisha was driven away by a woman chauffeur in uniform. The Premier went from Downing Street to Buckingham Palace where he stayed with the King for three quarters of an hour.

It was announced last night that as from September 16 all petrol will be rationed. In the meantime all car owners are asked not to use their cars more than is vitally necessary.

Today all banks throughout Britain will be closed

Australia yesterday declared war on Germany. "Where Britain stands, stand the people of the Empire and the British world," said Prime Minister Menzies in a broadcast message last night.

New Zealand has cabled her full support to Britain. There is a rush of recruits in Canada. At Toronto a queue of 2,000 men lined outside the Recruiting Office. Japan has assured Britain of her neutrality in the present war.

Britain's last two-hour ultimatum to Germany was revealed to the people of Britain in a memorable broadcast from Downing Street by Mr Chamberlain at 11.15 yesterday morning. By that time Britain had been at war for fifteen minutes.

The House of Commons met at noon. The Premier spoke quietly to a grave, resolute House. He told of the ultimatum delivered in Berlin three hours before, of the assurances demanded from Germany before 11 am.

"No such undertaking was received by the time stipulated" Mr Chamberlain said, "Consequently his country is now at war with Germany."

Only once the Premier's voice trembled. "For no one," he said, with a trace of emotion in his voice, "has it been a sadder day than for me. Everything I worked for, everything I hoped for, everything I believed through my public life has crashed in ruins!" But now he was able to speak freely. "I trust I may live," he said, as the cheers resounded through the House, "To see the day when Hitlerism has been destroyed so as to restore the liberty of Europe."

"STAND CALM, UNITED WE SHALL PREVAIL":
THE KING

Seated alone in his study in Buckingham Palace, the King broadcast to his people last evening. In serious, measured tone, he said: "In this grave hour, perhaps the most fateful in our history, I send to every household of my people, both at home and overseas, this message, spoken with the same depth of feeling for each one of you as if I were able to cross your threshold and speak to you myself. For the second time in the lives of most of us we are at war. Over and over again we have tried to find a peaceful way out of the differences between ourselves and those who are now our enemies. "But it has been in vain. We have been forced into a conflict. For we are called, with our allies, to meet the challenges of a principle which, if it were to prevail, would be fatal to any civilised order in the world. It is the principle which permits a State, in the selfish pursuit of power, to disregard its treaties and its solemn pledges; which sanctions the use of force, or threat of force, against the sovereignty, and independence of other States." His voice rose a little, the pace of his words increased, as he declared: "Such a principle, stripped of all disguise, is surely the mere primitive doctrine that might is right; and if this principle were established throughout the world, the freedom of our country and of the whole British Commonwealth of Nations would be in danger.

Breaking Bondage of Fear

"But far more than this – the peoples of the world would be kept in the bondage of fear and all hopes of settled peace and of the security of justice and liberty among nations would be ended. This is it he ultimate issue which confronts us. For the sake of all that we ourselves hold dear, and of the world's order and peace, it is unthinkable that we should refuse to meet the challenge. It is to this high purpose that I now call my people at home and my peoples across the seas, who will make our cause their own. I ask them to stand calm and firm and united in this time of trial. The task will be hard. There may be dark days ahead, and war can no longer be confined to the battlefield. But we can only do the right as we see the right, and reverently commit our cause to God of one and all. If we keep resolutely faithful to it, ready for whatever service or sacrifice it may demand, then, with God's help, we shall prevail. May He bless and keep us all." The King wore the dark blue un-dress uniform of an Admiral of the Fleet. As he spoke, the Queen listened in another room. When Britain entered the war at eleven o'clock, the King and Queen were together in their private rooms at the Palace.

Reproduced courtesy of Mirror newspaper group

ABEL B
Royal Observer Corps, Bearsted

ABERY E A
Special Constable

ADAMS ROBERT
1 Yew Tree Villas, Plantation Lane
Royal Navy

AKEHURST HAROLD
Hollebeke, Ashford Road

APPLETON CHARLES R
5 Council Houses, The Street

APPS WILLIAM G
2 The Cottages, Chapel Lane, Ware Street

ASHBEE PAUL
Four Walls, Spot Farm Estate
Royal Electrical and Mechanical Engineers

ATKINS DAPHNE M
Sunways, The Grove

ATTWOOD LEWIS

AUSTIN N E
Little Budds, Thurnham
Royal Artillery

AVARD JOHN A G G
23 Royston Road

AYRES ARTHUR
Ware Street

AYRES C R
Glencoe, Royston Road
Army

AYRES HERBERT T
Rose Cottages, Ware Street

BACON GEOFFREY
Edensor, Ashford Road
Royal Marines

BACON STEWART C J
Conrace, Ashford Road
Royal Air Force

BACON WILLIAM

BAILY KENNETH L M
Hill House, Ware Street

BAKER CLAUDE
Swaylands, Yeoman Lane
Royal Navy

BAKER ERNEST J
Holly Tree Cottage, Weavering Street

BAKER H R
Olde Highgate, Plantation Lane

BAKER JACK

After war was declared, petrol rationing was also announced. Only essential workers in the community, such as doctors, would be entitled to a petrol ration, so many families put away their cars 'for the duration', little realising that it would be many years before the vehicles would be used again. However, some local garages realised that the petrol ration would go further if vehicles were adequately maintained, This advertisement appeared in the Kent Messenger, 30 September 1939:

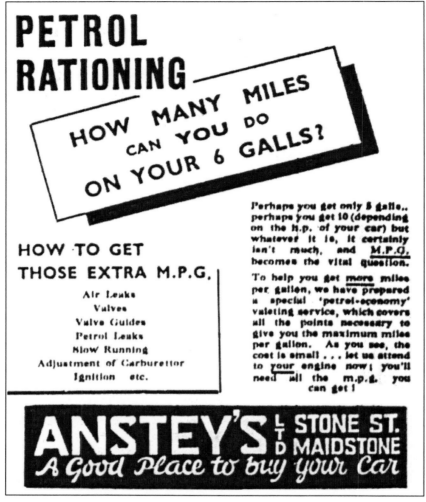

Reproduced courtesy of Kent Messenger group

The rationing brought increased administration as petrol pumps had to be read daily to ascertain sales, ration coupons had to be accounted and a daily form returned to the Ministry of Transport. Some garages took on contracts which assisted the war effort and employed local people. Shorts Brothers of Rochester agreed contracts with garages with machine shops. Parts for flying boats and other aircraft could be prepared, machined and assembled before being returned to the factory premises in the Medway area.

BAKER KENNETH
Ashview, Plantation Lane

BAKER ROBERT F
The Leas, Lord Romney's Hill

BAKER SUSAN

BAKER WILLIAM H
East Len, Spot Lane
Royal Marines

BAKER ------
East Len, Spot Lane
Coldstream Guards

BALDERSTONE BERNARD G
170 Royston Road

BARHAM ALBERT E
Sweetbriars, Yeoman Lane
Royal Corps of Signals

BARRATT FLORENCE
Court Farm Cottages, Thurnham Lane

BARRETT LESLIE D
Wooded Slopes, Detling

BARTON ERNEST H
5 Council Cottages, Spot Lane

BASELEY HENRY W
Bermuda, Royston Road

BATCHELLER RICHARD

BATCHELLER ROBERT M
The Little House, Roseacre Lane

BEALE STANLEY
40 Royston Road

BEDFORD REGINALD C F
Leevale, Ashford Road

BEDFORD REX

BEDOW STANLEY G C
217 Winifred Road

BEECHING A

BEECHING R J
Bydews, Weavering Street
Royal Air Force

BEECHING ------
Bydews, Weavering Street
Corps of Military Police

A transcript from the Kent Messenger, 2 September 1939:

If the Crisis Breaks....

POINTS YOU SHOULD REMEMBER

THEY SPELL SAFETY

We all hope that the present crisis will pass over as it has on previous occasions, but should it break, readers are reminded of the following points:

1   Gas masks should be handy – they should be carried to work. Everybody should already have fitted their gas masks so that they are comfortable to wear and so that if a newspaper or card is put over the bottom of the cylinder it is impossible to breathe: this shows that the gas mask is fitting correctly.

Remember time is the essence of the contract. It should be possible to find, put on and adjust your gas mask in six seconds. Try it on your family and on yourself!

One other point: don't take a long breath before putting your gas mask on – you might breathe in poisonous gas. When the gas mask is on, breathe out to eject any poisonous gas which may be inside the mask before you get it on.

2   Windows should be covered with a good thickness of cellophane paper or criss-crossed with gummed paper. If you haven't this, pasted brown paper will do. This will not prevent the window breaking but it will prevent the splinters flying. Skylights should be covered inside with wire netting so that glass doesn't fall on people below.

3   Bombs. Don't worry about high explosives. In one ten-thousandth of a second you will either be dead or alive. If you are dead there is nothing to worry about – if alive, thank God for it.

Gas Bombs. Probably very little gas will be used – the chief danger is from incendiary bombs. These should be tackled either by pouring sand on them or with a fine spray of water to make it burn out quickly. It will be up to those living in detached houses to see to the incendiary bombs themselves, for the fire brigade will specialise on the congested areas where there is danger of fire spreading. If an incendiary bomb falls in the garden, let it stop there and burn out of its own accord – it will be quite harmless.

In your dug out there should be a pick and shovel in case you should get trapped; wireless to keep you happy; and a loud gong or bell to attract attention should you be unable to get out. Of course, if there are two entrances, escape should be easy

4   Last of all, don't panic: the people in Spain got quite used to war dangers – it is always the first week which is the worst.

After All, It May Never Happen

Reproduced courtesy of Kent Messenger group

BEER EDWARD
2 Golf View Cottages, Ware Street

BENCE E W J
Milgate Park
Royal Artillery Major

BENNY RAYMOND

BENTLEY STANLEY C
Haifa, Roseacre Lane
Royal Air Force

Stanley qualified as a pilot. His service included postings to St Austell and Wales.

BETTS ALBERT S
Cobham Cottage, Water Lane

BETTS FRANK

BETTS SIDNEY

BIRCH JOHN P
Aldington Court Cottages
Royal Engineers

BISHOP JOHN S
Cobbins, The Grove

BLAMIRE BROWN C R
Southfield, Tower Lane

BLAMIRE BROWN JOHN
Southfield, Tower Lane
Royal Marines

BLANDFORD CYRIL E
The Green
Royal Army Medical Corps

BLANDFORD WILLIAM

BODIAM ELLEN F
1 Triangle Cottages, Yeoman Lane

BODIAM ROBERT W H
211 Winifred Road

BOTTLE HENLEY A
Maydene, Weavering Street

A transcript from the Kent Messenger, 9 September 1939:

WE CAN ALL HELP WIN THIS WAR

The war in which since Sunday the British Empire has been engaged will be won, or lost, not only in the field of battle, but in the homes of the people.

That is why, although we cannot all serve in the armed forces, every one of us can contribute in very real measure towards the victory which we are confident will be ours.

We can contribute by carrying on quietly with our jobs, being cheerful and keeping out heads.

The Germans have started this war with their people ignorant, bewildered, and hungry.

We have met their challenge with a stout heart, not only because we understand the issues and know we are fighting in a just cause, but because our larders are full, our resources plentiful.

We do not expect our lives to go on as usual. We are prepared to suffer inconvenience and danger, and we are proud to think that in some small measure we can in our own homes share the perils and hardships of our men who wage our war on land and sea and in the air.

By meeting our own problems with equanimity and cheerfulness, we are making their task more easy and doing our duty to our country and our cause.

Reproduced courtesy of Kent Messenger group

BOX GEORGE W A
Droglands, Ashford Road

BRADBEER HENRY J
Coombatch, The Landway

BRADLEY CYRIL B
Roseacre Farm

BRADLEY DENNIS R
Roseacre Farm

BRADLEY REGINALD

BRANSBY FREDERICK
Hazeldene, Spot Lane
Royal Air Force

BRIMSTED EDWARD E
The Green

BRITCHER THOMAS
The Queen's Own (Royal West Kent Regiment)

Thomas served as part of the British Army of the Rhine.

BROOK BENJAMIN B
White Horse Inn

BROOK BRIAN

BROWN ARTHUR

BROWN D J
6 Council Houses, The Street
Royal Navy

BROWN DAISY MURIEL
See entry for TEMPLE

BROWN HILDA

BROWN LAURIE

BROWN LUCY

BROWN MURIEL BEATRICE
See entry for FRISKEN

BUCK ROY D
Felderland, Ashford Road

BUCK TERENCE

BURCH ALBERT

BURGESS FREDERICK WILLIAM *
Single
Parents Nelson Henry and Ada Elsie Burgess of Invicta Villas
Royal Army Ordnance Corps
Service Number 7663330 Private
Died 28 August 1943, aged 26
Prisoner of War at Kuie Camp, Thailand
Buried in grave 6 B 45, Kancanaburi War Cemetery, Thailand

BURGESS RONALD N J
4 Invicta Villas, The Green
Royal Air Force

BURNYEAT DIANA

BUTLER ROY

BYAM ARTHUR A
Triangle Cottages, Yeoman Lane

CALCUTT P F
Sellindge, Plantation Lane
Royal Naval Volunteer Reserve

CAPELING FREDERICK E
Dromore, Cavendish Way

CARR ERNEST R
Ormonde, 215 Winifred Road
Royal Air Force

CARR HAROLD
Ashley, Ashford Road

CASTLE F
Service Number 4104959
53rd Reconnaissance Regiment

CHAINEY CHARLES A
Weston House, Spot Lane

CHANTLER JOHN

CHANTLER WILLIAM ERNEST *
Manor Rise
Married
Wife Iris May Chantler
Parents Edmund William and Olive Orpah Avery Chantler
Royal Artillery and 198th Light Anti Aircraft Regiment
Service Number 166849 Lieutenant
Died 15 February 1946, aged 30
Commemorated Panel 2, Column 2, Brookwood Memorial, Surrey

CHAPLIN CHAS. H A
199 Winifred Road

CHAPMAN JEAN M N
Sidcoombe, Ashford Road
Auxiliary Territorial Service

CHAWNER HARRY
1 May's Cottages, Ware Street

CHAWNER SIDNEY
1 May's Cottages, Ware Street
Royal Engineers

CHUBB ALFRED J
Brydale, Plantation Lane

CHUBB JAMES

As the international situation deteriorated, many companies began to produce goods that would be of use should war be declared. There were many different types of air raid shelter and window protection products that were available to buy, as these three advertisements which appeared in the Kent Messenger, 11 November 1939 show. The shelters were still very expensive to purchase. Many people used Anderson and Morrison shelters instead, and these became the best known designs. The windows of Bearsted School were protected with very fine gauge wire netting and the foundation stone was covered up as it included the names of local villages: Bearsted, Thurnham, Boxley and Detling.[1] An air raid shelter was not built at the school until November 1940.

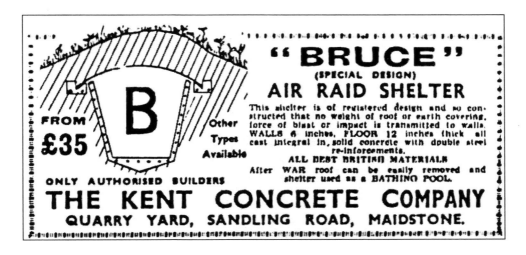

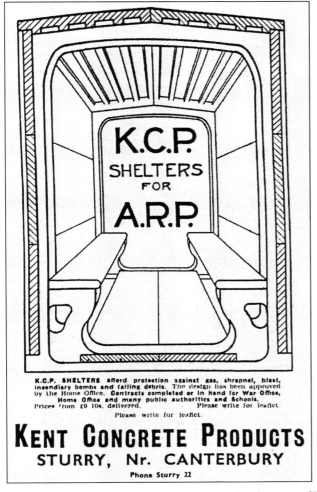

Reproduced courtesy of Kent Messenger group

This photograph appeared in the South Eastern Gazette, 28 July 1942, under the title: 'Minding the Kiddies whilst Mothers do their shopping'. The report continued 'In the garden room at Snowfield, Bearsted (home of Mrs Litchfield Speer), Red Cross, Kent 624 detachment , Girls Cadet Corps, are doing a valuable war-time job looking after babies whiles their mothers are shopping.'

Photograph courtesy of Kent Messenger group

Included in the photograph:

Back Row (Helpers):

Eileen Blandford; Billie Hilton; Margery Green; Betty Weaver; Doris Bentley; Margery Mercer; Audrey Marsh

Seated:

Betty Vane and Marion Smith

Children:

Susan Lee; Roger Smith (on lap); Gerald Hunt; Peter Hunt (on rocking horse); Doreen Vane; Kenneth Smith; Roy and Leslie Datson.

CLIFTON CHARLES B
Forteviot, Yeoman Lane

CLOUT VALLANCE
Little Dunkeld, Fauchons Lane

COALES JOHN WILLIAM *+
Briardene, Ashford Road
Single
Parents Edith and Herbert Coales
Royal Air Force Volunteer Reserve
35 Squadron
Service Number 1806859 Flight Sergeant (Pilot)
Died 27 June 1946, aged 21
Buried in grave 14 F2, Hanover War Cemetery, Niedersachsen, Germany

John was Captain of Bearsted School and Captain of Bertie House in 1938.[2] He went into accountancy in Maidstone after leaving school. Before the war, he joined the Royal Air Force Association which was aimed at people interested in aviation, but not specifically geared for war time flying.

After John joined the Volunteer Reserve he began flying on Tiger Moths before moving to Spitfire V, Meteor and Tempest aircraft. His service included duty in the Mediterranean and Bloemfontein in South Africa. He took part in the Victory Fly Past over Buckingham Palace with Douglas Bader on 8 June 1946, and paraded through Maidstone for the V J Celebrations.

John fatally crashed during an exercise which involved formation cross-country and low flying, in a Tempest V, over Wunsdorf, north of Osnabruck, Germany. It was some considerable time before it was realized that the crash was due to a mechanical failure of the aircraft rather than pilot error.

In 1999 Edith Coales took part in a war graves pilgrimage organised by the Royal British Legion. It began with lunch in the House of Lords and the Bishop of Manchester was the guest of honour. On 1 May 1999, Edith laid some flowers on John's grave and was able to say 'Goodbye': over half a century after her son's death.

This photograph shows John proudly showing his 'wings badge', after qualifying as a pilot:

Photograph courtesy of Edith Coales

COBB R ANTHONY
Beechdene, Ashford Road

COLEGATE CHARLES E
4 Fancy Row, Thurnham Lane

COLEGATE HERBERT

COLEGATE HERBERT G
Smarts Cottages, The Green

COLEGATE JOHN A
Smarts Cottages, The Green

COLLAR GLADYS

COLLINS HARRY
4 Cavendish Way

COOK PHILIP W
4 Egypt Place

COOKSON WALTER †
Married
Wife Joan Cookson
1/4th Battalion, Essex Regiment
Service Number 5569750 Corporal
Died 20 February 1944, aged 23
Buried in grave VII K 8, Cassino War cemetery, Italy
The entry on the Commonwealth War Graves Commission website gives a wrong first name: Walker

COOPER CHARLES E
2 West View, Roseacre Lane

COOPER CHARLES F
15 Pine Grove, Caring Lane
Royal Air Force

COOPER ------
Royal Observer Corps, Bearsted

CORAM LESLIE
6 Cavendish Way

CORFE ROGER

CORKE STANLEY

COSTIN HORN EDWARD A
The Cot, near Black Horse, Thurnham
Royal Engineers Major

COX ALAN E
1 The Gables, Lord Romney's Hill

COX STEPHEN
5 Mays Cottages, Ware Street

COX WILLIAM

CRAMPTON CYRIL
1 Holly Villas, The Street
Royal Air Force

CRANE ARTHUR T
11 Cavendish Way

CRASKE W L
The Haven, Lord Romney's Hill
Royal Engineers
Service Number 2196463 Lance Corporal

CRAVEN G
Manor Rise
Royal Navy Stoker

He was posted Missing, presumed killed, when H M S Electrum was sunk, but arrived in England, having been invalided home after a minor injury.

CRELLIN JENNIFER L
Stocks, Spot Lane

CROUCH LES
This undated photograph shows Les on the right with his friend, John Gilbert wearing Army uniform. They joined up on the same day.

Photograph courtesy of John E Gilbert

CROUCHER ALFRED H
44 Sandling Lane, Maidstone

CROWSLEY ERNEST G H
Newlands, Cavendish Way

CURTIS SYDNEY
4 Council Houses, The Street

DANIELL JOHN

DAVEY LIONEL
Yeoman House, Ashford Road
Royal Air Force

DAVIS HAROLD
2 Hill Cottages, Roseacre Lane

DAVIS TERENCE
Clover Rise, Fauchons Lane

DAWE JEAN D
Vicarage Cottages, Thurnham

DEARING N
Royal Observer Corps, Bearsted

DELVES STANLEY

DENNIS W F

DICKENSEN CHAS. J
3 Oliver's Row
Royal Engineers

DICKER STANLEY J
5 Pine Grove

DONALDSON ALLEN

DRAKE CYRIL
The Poplars, Ashford Road
Royal Navy

DRAPER CYRIL

DRUMMOND KINGSLEY
Ashley House, Bell Field, Weavering

DUNLAP MICHAEL L
Oaklands, Thurnham Lane
Army

DURBAN HARRY E
Milgate Lodge, Ashford Road

EALHAM G F
Royal Army Medical Corps Corporal

EARL HAROLD

EARL HENRY GEORGE
6 Fancy Row, Thurnham Lane

EARL S F
Ware Street
Royal Artillery

EATON-SHORE EILEEN VENABLES (née Lewis)
Women's Auxiliary Air Force Leading Aircraft Woman
Madginford Farm House

Eileen married John Holt Eaton-Shore, a Flight Lieutenant of the Royal Air Force, from Cheshire in 1945.

EAVES THOMAS D
Ashmore, Ashford Road

EDMONDS FRANK
Church Farm, Ashford Road

EGAN JOHN
Lisgibbon, Ashford Road

ELGAR CHARLES ROBINSON *
Married
Wife Esme Elgar of Swanage, Dorset
Parents Walter Robinson and Lilian Elgar
Royal Air Force (Auxiliary Air Force)
Service Number 90009 Squadron Leader (Pilot)
Died 22 May 1943, aged 32
Buried in grave 4, Row 9, St Bartholomew's churchyard, Bobbing

Charles was organist at Holy Cross church, Bearsted and lived on the Green.

ELLIS BASIL H
Roysden, Roundwell
The Queen's Own (Royal West Kent Regiment)

ELSWOOD ALBERT L
3 Egypt Place

ELVES STANLEY R
6 Mote Villas, The Green
Royal Navy

EVERSDEN RICHARD A
Holly House, The Street

EVERSDEN STEPHEN H
Holly House, The Street
Royal Army Service Corps

FARMER JOHN E A
Babbacombe, The Grove

FAULKENER LEONARD S B
Yonder Cottage, Tower Lane

FAULKENER Mrs W M
Yonder Cottage, Tower Lane
Women's Auxiliary Air Force

Mrs Faulkener was the first woman to leave Bearsted on 4 September 1939 to join the forces after war was declared.

FELLOWES SIDNEY HUBERT
Mill Cottage, Willington

FILMER WILLIAM G
Sutton Street

FINNEGAN JAMES P
2 West View, Roseacre Lane

FINNIS CYRIL F
Morningside, The Grove
Royal Army Ordnance Corps

FLOOD ALBERT

FLOOD B W
Ware Street

FLOOD GEORGE
2 Neatherton Cottages, Ware Street

FOGG-ELLIOTT MARK
Danedale, Church Lane
Royal Navy
Commander H M S Delight
Companion to Distinguished Service Order 1940 (London Gazette, July 1940)

FORWARD STANLEY J
Oak Cottage

FOSTER VIOLET L
Rosherville, The Green

FOX CHARLES
4 The Cottages, Chapel Lane
The Buffs (East Kent Regiment)

FOX JAMES

FRANKLIN-BATES RONALD H
2 Yew Tree Villas, Plantation Lane

FRENCH JAMES S
Glennifer, Roseacre Lane

FREESTONE WILLIAM G
Milford, Lord Romney's Hill

FRISKEN MURIEL BEATRICE (née Brown)
6 Council Houses, The Street
Auxiliary Territorial Services Lance Corporal

Muriel married John Frisken, Private, 2nd New Zealand Expeditionary Force in 1945

FROST CHARLES HENRY DENNIS *
Single
Parents William Henry and Dorothy Beaumont Frost
Royal Air Force Volunteer Reserve
Service Number 910014 Sergeant (Wireless Operator, Air Commander)
Died 27 March 1941, aged 22
Buried Holy Cross churchyard, Bearsted
Charles is also commemorated on a panel, west pavilion of Charing crematorium.

A transcript of the report from the Kent Messenger, 5 April 1941:

Photograph courtesy of Kent Messenger group

Death of Sergt. C.H.D. Frost

Great sympathy is felt for Mr W.H. Frost, Estates Manager to Maidstone Corporation, and with Mrs Frost, in the loss of their only son, Sergt. Charles Henry Dennis Frost, R.A.F., on Thursday of last week, of which they have received official news. Sergt. Frost, who was 22 years of age, joined the Royal Air Force December 19th 1939, and had therefore been on war service for the past 15 months. Educated at Maidstone Grammar School, he left about five years ago and entered the service department of the Maidstone Corporation Electricity Undertaking.

The funeral took place on Thursday from his home at Ribblesdale, Milgate, Bearsted, for interment at Bearsted Church. The service was conducted by the Rev R A Parsons, Vicar of Bearsted.

FRY TREVOR
Single
Royal Air Force.
Distinguished Flying Cross

FULLAGER HUBERT H
4 West View, Roseacre Lane

FULLER ALBERT W
Cherwell, Ashford Road

GARDNER REGINALD GEORGE *
Ware Street
Married
Wife Nancy Gardner
Parents Samuel and Agnes Gardner
Royal Air Force Volunteer Reserve
608 Squadron
Service Number 68776 Flight Lieutenant (Pilot)
Died 9 October 1944, aged 31
Buried in grave 184, Section N, at Holy Cross churchyard, Bearsted

Flight Lieutenant Gardner was flying with O C Sweetman, Navigator (Distinguished Flying Medal) in a Mosquito aircraft which was returning from Germany. As they neared their Norfolk base, Downham Market, the aircraft started to fall at a thousand feet and exploded on the ground at 21.30 hours. O C Sweetman was buried in Newcastle upon Tyne.

A partial transcript of the report from the Kent Messenger, 20 October 1944:

Photograph courtesy of Kent Messenger group

FLT.-LIEUT. REGINALD GARDNER

Funeral at Bearsted

The funeral took place on Monday, at Holy Cross Church, Bearsted, of Flt. Lieut. Reginald George Gardner, aged 31. The Rev E M Hughes (priest in charge and a late R A F chaplain) conducted the service.

Chief mourners were: Mrs R Gardner (widow), Mrs F Gardner (mother), Mrs J Sorrell (sister), Mr and Mrs A Williamson and Mrs L Secker (cousins). Flt. Lieut. Lilley represented his R.A.F. station and Mr R Smith represented the Puck-a-Pu band.

Flt. Lieut. Gardner's brother, Corporal J Gardner, was unable to attend the funeral owing to the fact that he is on active service on north west Europe.

GAULD KENNETH M
Puckscroft, The Landway
Suffolk Regiment

GEE DANIEL S
Ware Street

GEE SIDNEY

GIBBENS ERNEST W
Crompton, Fauchons Lane

GILBERT CYRIL

GILBERT FRANK W
Parks Cottages, Ware Street

GILBERT JOHN ALAN †*+
Ware Street
Married
Wife Bessie Letitia Gilbert of Hollingbourne
Son John Edward Gilbert
Parents Charles Edward and Amy Gilbert
4th Battalion, The Queen's Own (Royal West Kent Regiment)
Service Number 6346570 Lance Corporal
Died 10 January 1944, aged 25
Buried in grave 12 B 11, Taukkyan War Cemetery, Burma (now Myanmar)
John is also commemorated on the war memorial at Hollingbourne.

These photographs show John and Bessie on their wedding day and a recent photograph of John's grave.
John Edward was only two when his father died. John's family arrange for a cross or wreath of poppies to
be laid every year on his grave at Taukkyan.

Photographs courtesy of John E Gilbert

GILBERT WILLIAM A
Parks Cottages, Ware Street
Bombardier

GILES WILLIAM MONTAGUE C
3 Golf View Cottages, Ware Street
Bombardier

After the war, William helped to organise the Welcome Home arrangements for Bearsted and Thurnham.
He was Chairman of Thurnham parish council 1964-1966.

GODDARD NORMAN E
Three Stacks, Landway

GOLDSMITH LEONARD

GOLDTHORPE GAVIN

GOLDUP NELLIE
4 Roseacre Terrace, Tower Lane
Auxiliary Territorial Service

GOODHEW JOHN H
The Clayton, The Grove

GOODMAN GERALD
Hill Top, Tower Lane

GOOSEMAN JOHN F
Hyeres, The Landway

GRAINGER STUART

GRANT ALBERT R
1 The Cottages, Chapel Lane

GRANT D
1 The Cottages, Chapel Lane
Royal Marines

GRANT FREDERICK G C
Sunny Villa, Manor Rise

GREGORY R
Hill View
Mr Gregory trained many members of the Local Defence Corps.

GRIFFITHS DAPHNE A
Moorings, Lord Romney's Hill

GRIFFITHS HUGH

GROUT F
Royal Observer Corps, Bearsted

GROUT GORDON W T
West View, Thurnham Lane
Army

GUEST ALFRED HERBERT
Keeper's Cottage, Thurnham Lane

GUEST ERNEST JOHN
Keeper's Cottage, Thurnham Lane

GUEST REGINALD JAMES
Keeper's Cottage, Thurnham Lane

GUEST ROBERT GEORGE †
Married
Wife Cissy Lily Guest, of Catford, London
Parents Walter William and Rose Guest of Thurnham
Royal Navy
Service Number C/JX 127267 Able Seaman
His Majesty's Motor Torpedo Boat 310
Died 14 September 1942, aged 31
Commemorated 54; 2, Chatham Naval Memorial
Distinguished Service Medal.

Torpedo boats were used to for silent search and ambushes of German shipping routes. The engines were used to enable the boat to escape at a very fast speed. Each boat carried two torpedoes and four machine guns. The nature of this warfare with this type of boat was rapid and intense: success often hinged on a split-second decision. Many of the crews were awarded medals for their actions and bravery.

HADLEY HENRY
Otteridge Cottage, Yeoman Lane

HAGGER GILBERT

HALLETT A E
4 May's Cottages, Ware Street
Royal Artillery

HALMETT A

HAMMERTON KENNETH
Car-Trav, Ashford Road
Kenneth was a prisoner of war.

HAMMOND CHAS. W H
Meadow View, Lord Romney's Hill

This undated photograph was taken during a wartime parade and service held on the Green, Bearsted in 1942. The parade included members of the civil defence forces, armed forces, Holy Cross church choir, 1st Bearsted Girl Guides, Air Raid Precaution wardens, Red Cross, Kent 226 detachment, and Junior Red Cross, Kent 524 detachment:

Photograph courtesy of Jenni Hudson

HAMMOND EBENEZER *
Triangle Cottages, Yeoman Lane
Married
Wife Alice Amelia Hammond
Civilian drayman at Maidstone West Station
Died 3 August 1944, aged 57
Listed on the civilian section of the Roll of Honour for the Municipal Borough of Maidstone

HAMMOND FRANK H
The Rose Inn, Ashford Road

HAMSON ERNEST

HARDING A G
Holly Tree Cottage, Weavering
Royal Engineers

HARDY JOHN K
Home Cottage, Roundwell
Royal Electrical and Mechanical Engineers

HARNETT CHARLES H
Rockies, Yeoman Lane

HARNETT EDWARD F
Roseridge, Roseacre Lane
Army Lieutenant

HARNETT F
Royal Observer Corps, Bearsted

HARRIS ERIC S
Mooltan, Ashford Road
Royal Artillery

HARRIS FAITH S
Cherrydene, Roseacre Lane

In the early stages of the war, the government placed great emphasis on achieving thoroughly darkened streets. It was hoped that it would therefore be difficult for enemy planes to gain bearings from landmarks, outlines of urban areas, and other significant buildings or structures on the ground. However, nothing could be done about the distinctive shape of the river Thames as it led a way up to London from the sea! If there was a breach of 'black-out' regulations, households were liable to fines. One of the simplest ways of blocking out light was to put up curtains or panels made from black-out fabric when twilight began in the evening. This advertisement for black-out material appeared in the Kent Messenger, 30 September 1939:

Reproduced courtesy of Kent Messenger group

HARRIS MONTAGUE
Frantom, Plantation Lane

HARRISON BETTY FRANCES
See entry for VAUGHAN

HARRISON THOMAS †

HARVEY HENRY W
42 Roseacre Lane

HAWKINS ERIC
The Bungalow, Mote Hall
Royal Air Force

HEAD PEGGY
173 Royston Road

HEARD ANTHONY J C
Cherisy, Ashford Road

HEARD ROWLEY
The Willows

HEIGHTON RONALD A
Plumstones, The Grove

HEWETT F L
Clarendon, Roseacre Lane

HEWETSON BRIAN G
203 Winifred Road

HEWETSON PETER A
Holmleigh, Roseacre Lane

HICKMOTT DESMOND J
1 Egypt Place
Prisoner of War

HICKMOTT RONALD H
1 Egypt Place

HIGGENS HENRY B
Amesbury, Spot Farm Estate
Royal Navy

HILL WILLIAM J
Earlsfield House, Spot Lane
Royal Air Force

HILL WILLIAM R
Toys Hill, Spot Farm Estate
Royal Electrical and Mechanical Engineers

HILLS ARTHUR A
The Orchard, Lord Romney's Hill

HIRST BERNARD E
6 Roseacre Terrace, Tower Lane

HOLMES GEORGE R
Coronel, Royston Road
Royal Navy

HOLTUM A H
Special Constabulary Sergeant

HOLTUM ARTHUR J
Sunnycot, Roseacre Lane

HOLTUM KEITH R
Sunnycot, Roseacre Lane

HORN DUDLEY CROFTON *
Single
Parents Cyril Roland and Sarah Marion Horn
Royal Air Force Volunteer Reserve
247 Squadron
Service Number 1333758 Flight Sergeant (Pilot)
Died 14 January 1945, aged 21
Buried in the south west corner of Bergharen Protestant churchyard, Gelderland, Netherlands

HORN ------
Triangle Cottages
Auxiliary Territorial Services

HOWARD CECIL
Homeleigh, Yeoman Lane
Royal Air Force

HOWARD HARRY C
The Retreat, The Green
Royal Navy

Harry's naval service included H M S Chitral, His Majesty's Motor Torpedo Boats in Malta 1943 and H M S Gadfly 1945 before being discharged in 1946. This photograph shows Harry as a Chief Petty Officer in Malta:

Photograph courtesy of Jenni Hudson

HUBDEN N

HUBER W
10 Council Houses, The Street
Army

In June 1941 the Board of Trade published regulations for clothing and introduced a scheme called Civilian Clothing Control 1941. Clothes were now subject to ration coupons and government regulations. New garments had to be sold with a 'utility label and mark'. This came to be known as the CC41 mark.

The population was urged to 'Make Do and Mend' in a government booklet that gave hints and tips on repairing and renovating clothes. The aim of the booklet was to try to ensure that people were making the best of the clothes they already possessed. Readers were urged to consider home dressmaking, renovating old garments and other crafts; although many of the materials required were subject to wartime restrictions.

This photograph appeared in a contemporary dressmaking manual and depicted a fashionable young woman enjoying a worthwhile pastime.

Photograph courtesy of Malcolm Kersey

However, not everyone possessed the necessary time and patience to develop dressmaking skills and there was a limit to what could be renovated and refurbished. A new 'utility' range of clothes was introduced by the government following a collaborative project with fashion designers including Norman Hartnell, and Hardy Amies.

The first utility dress to be produced was designed by Hartnell. With great foresight, the government was aware of the historic nature of the dress and donated it to the Victoria and Albert museum, where it is still regularly displayed.

Many women were now employed in war work and factories, so there was a demand for sensible and safe clothing. Chiesmans store in Maidstone was quick to respond to their customers requirements as this advertisement which appeared in the Kent Messenger, 15 August 1941, shows:

Reproduced courtesy of Kent Messenger group

HULKS JOHN C
191 Winifred Road
Royal Navy

HUMPHREY JOSEPH T
La France, Roseacre Lane

HUMPHREYS MARISE JACQUELINE
See entry for RELF

HUNT ANTHONY G
Egypt House

HUNT JESSE G †
Friningham Cottages
Parents Mr and Mrs George Hunt of Cobham Cottage
Civilian War Dead
Died 13 August 1940, aged 37
Commemorated on Civilian Roll of Honour, Rural District of Hollingbourne

Jesse died during an air raid on Detling Aerodrome by Messerschmitt and Junkers aircraft. Twenty Anson aircraft and many of the buildings were destroyed. Over sixty members of the Royal Air Force and Women's Auxiliary Air Force were killed, including the Station Commander Group Captain E Davis.

HUNT HUBERT A
Tower Cottage, Tower Lane

HUNT VERA M
Aldington

HUNT WILLIAM F
Ivy House, The Green
Army

HUNTER GEORGE A
Marie Paule, The Landway

HUNTLEY WILLIAM S
The Kentish Yeoman

HURST CLIFTON E S
Yeoman House, Ashford Road

HUTTON STANLEY J
Green Bank, Fauchons Lane

INGRAM JAMES

IRWIN BROMLEY F S
The Green

JAMES ARTHUR G
Northgate, Ashford Road

JAMES KENNETH A
14 Spot Farm Estate
Royal Electrical and Mechanical Engineers

JESSEL RICHARD F
Mote House
Royal Navy

JOHNSON EDWARD

JOHNSON FLORENCE
Thurnham Court Cottages
Women's Auxiliary Air Force

JOHNSON WALTER J
Friningham Cottages

JONES MARGARET OSWALD
Snowfield Cottage
Women's Royal Naval Service

JONES RONALD R
167 Royston Road

KEAY EDWARD THOMAS JOSEPH *+
5 Council Houses, The Street
Single
Parents Edward William and Elizabeth Keay
Royal Air Force Volunteer Reserve
195 Squadron
Service Number 1896361 Sergeant
Died 23 November 1944, aged 20
Commemorated Panel 232, Runnymede Memorial, Surrey

Eddie was Captain of Bearsted School for two years and Captain of Fludd house.[3] He joined the Royal Air Force Volunteer Reserve and became a Flight Engineer with 195 Squadron.

His squadron had originally been formed at Duxford, Cambridgeshire, November 1942. It was re-formed in October 1944. From November 1944, the squadron was based at Wratting Common, Cambridgeshire.

Eddie's Lancaster Bomber took off on 23 November from RAF Witchford, Wratting Common at 1256hrs for a raid on Gelsenkirchen, Germany. On the way to Germany the aircraft caught fire and crashed into the sea, west of the Dutch island of Walcheren. All the crew members were reported as missing.

From the Bomber Command diary:

> 23 November 1944
> 168 Lancaster planes of No. 3 Group carried out a GH (*anti-radar*) bombing raid through cloud on the Nordstein oil plant at Gelsenkirchen (*near Essen, Germany*). The bombing appeared to be accurate. One Lancaster plane was lost, registration HK683.

This photograph of Edward accompanied an undated press cutting which reported his loss:

Photograph courtesy of Irene Bourne

Robert Skinner, headmaster of Bearsted school wrote this tribute when Eddie was posted Missing. It was published in the Parish Magazine:[4]

EDDIE KEAY - A TRIBUTE

Eddie Keay, one of the most popular of Bearsted school head boys and captains, is reported missing from an operational flight over enemy territory.

Eddie Keay was one of the finest and most likeable characters at Bearsted school, which he attended from 1933 to 1939. Always courteous and considerate, and as captain for two very successful pre-war years, he was an inspiration to the school and a great help to the staff. A terrific worker, and with a magnificent physique, at the age of 13, he led his sports teams to victory, and during those two years Bearsted School more than held its own with the schools in the district.

His school work was as outstanding as his physical activities. Always thorough and painstaking, he was quick to grasp new matters, and was one of the best scholars. It was no surprise to us who knew him that he was able to pass all his difficult Flight Engineer's examinations and pass into the Air Force a member of an air crew. Eddie never lost contact with us; on every leave he would visit the school to glance at the old groups in which he was such a prominent figure and to take his cheerful and confident smile through the rooms. His old fellow scholars will always remember that smile and the quiet confidence behind it.

The school prays that he may be returned to continue a life which is so full of promise. If that cannot be, we know that Eddie met whatever happened as he always met other things with a quiet calm – and without complaint.

Reproduced courtesy of Holy Cross church, Bearsted

There is a school prize in Eddie's name, donated by his sister, Mrs Irene Bourne which was first awarded at Roseacre School in 2003.

KEAY EDWARD WILLIAM
5 Council Houses, The Street

KEMBALL VERO

KENNEDY NORMAN W
Orchardene, The Grove

KENNETT FRANK E
Crisfield Cottage

KING DONALD G
4 Castle Cottages
Royal Navy

KING EDWARD ARTHUR
4 Castle Cottages
Royal Navy

Edward married Joyce Lavinia Harvey, Women's Auxiliary Air Force of 12 Cranston Gardens, Chadwell, Rochford, in 1941

KING GORDON D
4 Castle Cottages
Royal Navy

KING JOHN S
4 Castle Cottages
Royal Navy

KING LEONARD CHARLES
4a Fancy Row, Thurnham Lane

KING PERCY M
Kaypers, Royston Road

KING PHILIP W
Paget, Spot Lane
Royal Navy Captain

KINNE CECIL
St Mary's, Ashford Road

KIRBY WILLIAM E
1 Cavendish Way

KITCATTE CHARLES FREDERICK *
The Street
Married
Wife Gwendolyn Edith Kitcatte (née Jones)
Parents Robert George and Bertha Sarah Kitcatte (née Waller)
1st Battalion, Suffolk Regiment
Service Number 5825322 Sergeant
Died 4 June 1943, aged 30
Buried in grave 42, Plot 9, Row 3, Oostende New Communal Cemetery, West-Vlaanderen, Belgium

KNIGHT ALBERT W
1 Rosemary Road
Royal Artillery

KNIGHT STANLEY G
1 Rosemary Road

KREJSA SIDNEY R H
Carsphairn, The Grove

LAMLEY FRANK P
1 Golf View Cottages, Ware Street

LAMSLEY ARTHUR H
Bengalah, 206 Winifred Road

LANG FRANCIS H

LATTIN CHARLES H
Applegarth, The Landway

LAWRENCE GEORGE HENRY *
Lilk Mount, Otham Lane
Married
Wife Pamela Ianthe (née Thorpe)
Parents Henry (deceased) and Julia Lawrence (née Pearson-Remedios), 106 Ferry Road, APT1, Shanghai
Royal Canadian Air Force
628 (Royal Air Force) Squadron
Service Number J/5674 Flight Lieutenant
Died 3 March 1944, aged 27
Commemorated Column 441, Kranjii War Cemetery, Singapore
George is also commemorated on a separate memorial stone on Pamela's grave in Holy Cross churchyard, Bearsted. It gives an incorrect age: 28.

George was born in Shanghai, China but held British citizenship. Between 1934 and 1940 he was part of the Shanghai Volunteer Corps. He held the rank of Sergeant Technician before leaving to enlist in the Royal Canadian Air Force in Vancouver, Canada. He was awarded the 1937 Shanghai Emergency medal.

His wartime service included postings to Britain and duties at RAF Stations Leuchars and Aldergrove. On 15 August 1942, George married Pamela Thorpe at Holy Cross church, Bearsted. A transcript of the report from Kent Messenger, 21 August 1942:

Photograph courtesy of Kent Messenger group

F/O G. H. Lawrence, R.C.A.F.
Section Officer P. I. Thorpe, W.A.A.F. (Bearsted)

The wedding took place at Holy Cross Church., Bearsted, on Saturday of F/O George Henry Lawrence, R.C.A.F., son of the late Mr G.H.Lawrence and Mrs F.R.Crank, of Shanghai, China, and Section Officer P.I.Thorpe, W.A.A.F., daughter of Mr and Mrs Charles Thorpe, of Lilk Mount, Bearsted. The Rev R.A.F.Parsons officiated. The hymns sung were;- 'Lead us, Heavenly Father,', 'Praise my soul, the King of Heaven', and 'O Perfect Love.' Mr Ealham was at the organ. Given away by her father, Mr Charles Thorpe, the bride wore a gown of ivory satin beaute made on classic lines, the corsage embroidered in an original design of silver thread and glittering stones, with long, full skirt forming a train. The bridal veil of very handsome Brussels lace, lent by her mother, was surmounted by a coronet of orange blossom and the bride carried a sheaf of gladiolas and white heather. She was attended by her sister, Miss Monica Thorpe, and Miss Eileen Lewis, who wore blue velvet and net dresses with net and floral head-dresses and carried pink roses and little Miss Anne Lewis, a charming figure in white organdie and large poke bonnet, who carried a posy of blue and pink sweet peas. Pilot Officer K.Maffre, R.C.A.F., was best man and the ushers were Mr John C.Thorpe, brother of the bride, Fl./Lt. Armstrong, P/O L.Sharpe and Fl./Sgt Vokey.

The reception was held in the gardens of Lilk Mount. F/O and Mrs G.H.Lawrence left for their honeymoon at Liphook, the bride travelling in an ensemble of navy and Cambridge blue, with hat to match. The church was tastefully decorated by Mrs Charles Ambrose and friends. A guard of honour of W.A.A.F. was formed outside the church.

Pamela and George appear to be the only married couple from Bearsted and Thurnham to die in separate incidents whilst on active service during the war.

George was a passenger on board an aircraft, a Consolidated Catalina flying boat, Mark IB, registration BR357, which was flying overnight from Calcutta to China Bay, Ceylon (now Sri Lanka) on 3 March 1944. Although the departure from Calcutta was witnessed, the aircraft then disappeared and it was presumed to have come down in the Bay of Bengal. The subsequent investigation report mentioned that on the night of 3-4 March, a cyclone was recorded in the vicinity of the flight path but that the aircraft should have passed 120 miles east of the centre of it. On 5 March another Catalina, piloted by F L Godber, Squadron Leader and Commanding Officer of 628 Squadron, searched the area but found nothing. There seemed to be no reason for the loss of the aircraft other than abnormal weather conditions.

LAWRENCE PAMELA IANTHE (née Thorpe) *
Lilk Mount, Otham Lane
Married
Husband George Henry Lawrence
Parents Charles and Ettie Ianthe Thorpe of Lilk Mount
Women's Auxiliary Air Force, Dumfries, Scotland
Service Number 384 Flight Officer
Died 16 January 1943, aged 22
Buried in grave 23, Section J, Holy Cross churchyard, Bearsted
The headstone on Pamela's grave gives an incorrect date of death: 10 January 1943.

Pamela enlisted on 27 July 1939 and joined the Women's Auxiliary Air Force. In 1941 she was commissioned and held a temporary assignment as a section officer. In September 1942 she gained promotion to Flight Officer. She was killed in a flying accident on 16 January 1943.

Pamela was on board a Bristol Blenheim IV aircraft, registration Z7313, which was flying to Dumfries. The weather conditions were extremely poor. The aircraft flew into Laggan Hill, three miles south-west of Caulkerbush, Kirkcudbrightshire in Scotland. It struck the ground whilst on a steep turn to land and caught fire, later exploding. A subsequent investigation concluded that the flight was not sufficiently urgent to be undertaken in such bad weather and should have been abandoned earlier.

A partial transcript of the report from Kent Messenger, 29 January 1943:

Photograph courtesy of Kent Messenger group

W.A.A.F.s' TRIBUTE AT FUNERAL
Late Flight Officer Pamela Lawrence

Widespread regret is caused by the death of Flight Officer Pamela I.Lawrence, W.A.A.F., the 22 years-old daughter of Mr and Mrs C T Thorpe, of Lilk Mount, Ashford Road, near Maidstone, whose funeral took place on Friday at Bearsted, the Rev R.A.F.Parsons (vicar of Bearsted) and Squadron Leader the Rev Richard M.Taylor, R.A.F. officiating.

The funeral was held with full military honours, and quite a number of W.A.A.F.s in their smart blue uniforms were standing around the grave when the three volleys were fired.

Chief mourners were: Flight Lt G.H.Thorpe (husband), Mr and Mrs Charles T.Thorpe (mother and father), A.C.W.2 Monica Thorpe and John Thorpe (sister and brother), Mr Arthur Chattey and Miss Avis Chattey (aunt and uncle) and Srgt.Obs.H.H.Lawrence, R.A.F.

LEADBETER PERCY
Bredgar, The Grove

LEE THOMAS R
The Retreat, The Green
2nd Battalion, Royal Warwickshire Regiment
Company Quarter Master Sergeant
Thomas was a Prisoner of War in Stalag VIII B, Germany 1940 to 1945

This photograph shows Thomas in his uniform:

Photograph courtesy of Jenni Hudson

This undated photograph was taken at an open air service held on the Green at Bearsted during the war. Among the congregation can be seen many members of the Royal Air Force who travelled down from Detling aerodrome to attend the service:

Photograph courtesy of Jenni Hudson

LEWIS EILEEN VENABLES
See entry for EATON-SHORE

LEWIS JOHN
Hilltop Cottage, Roseacre Lane

LEWIS PAMELA

LEWIS RICHARD

LIELL JOHN

LIELL LAWRENCE J
Yelverton, Plantation Lane

LING EDWARD A
Sarum, Roseacre Lane

LITCHFIELD FREDERICK P
Bearsted Cottage

LITCHFIELD LAURENCE

LITCHFIELD OLIVER
Snowfield
Coldstream Guards

LITCHFIELD RICHARD HILL SANDYS *
Snowfield
Single
Parents   Rear Admiral F Shirley Litchfield-Speer, (Companion of the Order of St Michael and St George,
           Distinguished Service Order) and Cecilia Litchfield-Speer
Royal Navy Lieutenant
H M Australian Ship Parramatta
Died 27 November 1941, aged 26
Commemorated 41; 1, Chatham Naval Memorial

LITCHFIELD-SPEER JOHN S S
Snowfield
Royal Navy

LOCKYER FREDERICK †
Married
Wife Cicely Nellie Lockyer of Maidstone
Mother Gertrude Lockyer of 8 Hardy Street, Maidstone, formerly of The Rose Inn, Bearsted
53rd Tipper Company, Royal Army Service Corps
Service Number T/14668408 Driver
Died 28 January 1946, aged 36
Buried in grave X 33 28, Brussels Town Cemetery, Evere, Vlaams-Brabant, Belgium

A transcript of the report from Kent Messenger, 9 February 1946:

DIED IN BRUSSELS
Pte. F. H. Lockyer, R.A.S.C.

Official news of the death in Brussels of Pte. Frederick Henry Lockyer, R.A.S.C. on January 29th has been received by Mrs Lockyer, 8 Hardy Street, Maidstone. He was the son of the late Mr and Mrs Lockyer of the Rose Inn, Bearsted, where he was born.

Pte. Lockyer who was 36, spent all his two years service in the Army overseas. He left for the continent three weeks after D-Day.

Before joining the forces he worked at the Mid-Kent Laundry, Boxley Road. He was also an agent for the Liverpool Victoria Insurance Co., King Street. A widow and two daughters are bereaved.

LONG Mrs
7 Council Houses, The Street
Auxiliary Territorial Service

LONG BASIL N
7 Council Houses, The Street
Wiltshire Regiment

LONG JOHN

LONKHURST STANLEY L
Eryl, Roseacre Lane

LOYD JOHN C
Wendings, Roseacre Lane

LUXFORD A
Bell Lane, Ware Street
Women's Auxiliary Air Force

LUXFORD CHARLES
Bell Lane, Ware Street
Royal Artillery

MACKELDEN LESTER A
Vicarage Cottage, Thurnham Lane

MACKIE RAMSEY W M
Shenstone, Ashford Road

MACKNAY BASIL R F
Carnlea, Lord Romney's Hill

MACIVER JOHN CHRISTIAN *
9 Downside Crescent, Hampstead, London
Married
Wife Joyce MacIver
Parents Reverend Peter and Mrs MacIver, Bowmore, Islay, Argyllshire, Scotland
Civilian
Died 20 April 1941, aged 47 at Aldington South Court, Thurnham
Listed on Civilian Section of the Roll of Honour for the District of Hollingbourne

MANNING SIDNEY F
Mansfield, The Grove

MARGETTS JOAN
3 Church Lane
Auxiliary Territorial Service

MARSHALL JOHN C
Sellindge, Plantation Lane

MARTIN FREDERICK E
Oak Cottage, Ware Street

MARTIN WILLIAM W
Amebury, Lord Romney's Hill

MARWOOD ERNEST W
Llewellyn, Spot Farm Estate

MATTHEWS D J
Roseacre Stores, Ashford Road
Royal Navy

MATTHEWS PERCIVAL
Roseacre Stores, Ashford Road
Royal Air Force Sergeant-Pilot

MATTHEWS RICHARD

MAY ARTHUR L
11 Council Houses, The Street

A transcript of a report from the Kent Messenger, 24 July 1942:

Photograph courtesy of Kent Messenger group

GLAD NEWS FOR WIFE
Thurnham Man Reported Missing,
Now In Hospital

One of the eleven men of the Maidstone contingent of the R.A.M.C. who came back from Dunkirk, was Pte. Arthur May. He is 26 and in January last year, he married Miss M Seager of Bell Lane, Thurnham.

Recently his wife received news that he was missing in he Middle East since June 14th. On Wednesday of this week, Mrs May received a letter from her husband in a base hospital, dated June 25th. He joined the Maidstone Territorials in 1936 and before the war was employed at Messrs. Harnett's Nurseries, Bearsted.

McKEOUGH RAYMOND A
Rostrevor, Ashford Road
Royal Navy

McLONEGAL ------
Royal Observer Corps, Bearsted

MELLOR HAROLD

MERRITT HORACE G
Newcot, Weavering

MILDREN ERNEST S
Hatherill, Roseacre Lane
Royal Navy

MILDREN JOSEPH JACK
Hatherill, Roseacre Lane
Royal Air Force
Distinguished Flying Medal

MILES W

MILLER JOHN S, jun.
Dulwich, Royston Road

MILLER ROBERT G
Neatherton Cottages, Ware Street

MILNER PETER W A
Bandra, Royston Road

MITCHELL BRIAN

MONCKTON FRANCIS P
Maybank, The Green

MONCKTON JOHN
Royal Air Force

MONCKTON LANCE R S
Bell House, The Green
Royal Observer Corps, Bearsted

Lance was Chairman of Bearsted parish council, 1952-1960.

MOODY FRANK L J
Rougemont, Weavering Street

MOORE ALBERT
Royal Army Service Corps
Service Number S/10668415 Corporal

MOORE ROBERT
Dove Row, Royston Road
Grenadier Guards

MOORY F

MORLING MAURICE B
Two Trees, The Landway

MORRIS ARTHUR E
194 Winifred Road

MOSELEY WILLIAM E
Bletchingley, Weavering Street
Royal Artillery

MOSS B
Royal Observer Corps, Bearsted

MOSS NOEL
Ivy Dene, Thurnham Lane
Royal Air Force

MOTTON JOHN A
Ondeen, Spot Farm Estate

MOUNT DOUGLAS
Nine Elms, Hockers Lane
Army

MUNN ALAN V
Rosemead, Roseacre Lane

NAYLOR MARGARET L
1 Sunnyside, The Street

NEIL FREDERICK
184 Royston Road

NEWSHAM FLORENCE
See entry for PLUMMER

NOURSE ALEXANDER
Cambria, Ashford Road

O'GORMAN MERVYN J
197 Winifred Road
Royal Artillery

OLD GORDON G
Red Pillars, Ashford Road

OSBORNE RONALD
Chine Wood, Fauchons Lane
Royal Artillery

OSWALD R
Nether Milgate
Army

OVENDEN W

OVENDEN ------
Oak Dell, Weavering Street
Women's Auxiliary Air Force

PALMER EDWARD
Shirley Way

PALMER EDWARD W
Glendale, Spot Lane
Royal Navy

PALMER R A
Special Constabulary Sergeant

PALMER R C B
Fairview, The Green
Army

PANTING JOHN W
Snowfield Garage

PARKHOUSE CHARLES F
1 Council Houses, The Street

PARKIN WILLIAM HUGH *
Parents Mr and Mrs Whitehead of The Mount
Married
Son William Hugh Parkin
Royal Navy
Lieutenant Commander
Died 9 June 1940, aged 33 during sinking of H M S Glorious
Commemorated Bay 1, Panel 2, Lee on Solent Memorial, Hampshire, a memorial window to H M S Glorious in Holy Cross church, Bearsted and a memorial in St Peter's church, Martindale, Cumbria.

William came from a distinguished family: he was the son of Mr Whitehead who was the Under Sheriff of Kent. Mrs Whitehead came from the Parkin family of Westmorland and they lived at The Mount in Church Lane, Bearsted. William changed his surname to his mother's maiden name upon inheriting some of his grandfather's estate. He was a trained pilot and served on aircraft carriers before retiring in 1934. As a Royal Naval Reservist, he was recalled to active service in 1939 and posted to H M S Glorious.

H M S Glorious was one of the British war ships that provided cover for the evacuation of British, French and Polish forces from Narvik following the German invasion of Norway. At 4.30pm on 8 June, the Glorious and her two escorting destroyers, Acasata and Ardent, were sighted by the German battle cruisers Gneisenau and Scharnhorst which quickly opened fire on the British ships. The Ardent was soon sunk, but the Acasta continued to provide support for Glorious. Just after 6pm, Acasta and Glorious were overwhelmed. There was only one survivor from Acasta and fewer than forty from Glorious.

This photograph shows William in his naval uniform:

Photograph courtesy of Holy Cross church, Bearsted

Food rationing was introduced in January 1940, but not all foodstuffs were immediately restricted. The Ministries of Agriculture and Food worked together to ensure that the cultivation of land, food production and supply was maximised. The Ministries issued many leaflets. The intention was to give recipes and advice on how to produce nutritious and interesting meals for the family from the range of foods and rationed amounts that were available.

These transcribed details concern sandwich fillings and to modern tastes, appear quite startling:

Good sandwich fillings – have you tried these?

1   Mashed sardines, pilchards or herring mixed with shredded fresh carrot;

2   Vegetable or meat extract and mustard and cress;

3   Chopped cold meat with mashed cooked vegetables with seasoning;

4   Brawn, shredded swede and chutney.

Under the rationing scheme, an adult was entitled to a packet of dried egg every four weeks. These are the instructions on how to use this dehydrated food:

How to use Dried Egg:

1   Store the tin in a cool, dry place and replace the lid after use;

2   Mix one level tablespoon of the powder with two tablespoons of water;
This equals one fresh egg;

3   Treat this mixture as a fresh one;
Do not waste the mixture by making up more than is necessary for the dish; beat as usual before adding to other ingredients.

This recipe was named after Lord Woolton, who was Minister of Food:

Woolton Pie

Dice and cook 1lb of each of these vegetables: Potatoes, Cauliflower, Swedes, Carrots.

Strain the vegetables, but keep some of the water that was used to cook them. Place the vegetables in a large pie dish. Add a little vegetable extract and about an ounce of rolled oats or oatmeal to the vegetable liquid. Cook until liquid has thickened and pour over the vegetables. Add 3 – 4 spring onions.

Top with potato pastry or with mashed potatoes and heat in the centre of a moderately hot oven until golden brown.

Serves 4 to 6 people.

Reproduced courtesy of Malcolm Kersey

PARR NORMAN H
Anfield, The Landway

PAYNE ARTHUR G
The Haven, Lord Romney's Hill

PAYNE ROBERT W
Long Windows, The Grove

PEACH DENIS

PEARCE GEOFFREY B
Trevarno, Roseacre Lane
Royal Air Force

PEARSON FRANK
8 Council Houses, The Street
Royal Air Force

PERKESS JACK E
Tower Villa, Tower Lane

PELLETT ALBERT W
3 Invicta Villas, The Green

PELLETT GEORGE

PELLETT STANLEY

PENNELLS RONALD L
207 Winifred Road

PENNEY REGINALD LESLIE †
Single
Parents Thomas and Frances Ellen Penney of Maple Bar Gate, Thurnham
10th Battalion, Durham Light Infantry
Service Number 14688862 Private
Died 19 August 1944, aged 18
Buried in Banneville la Campagne War Cemetery, Calvados, France

Photograph courtesy of Trudy Johnson

PENNEY RONALD
Keeper's Cottage, Friningham
Royal Air Force

PENNEY STANLEY
Keeper's Cottage, Friningham
Royal Artillery

PILBEAM N E
4 Bearsted Spot
Army

PILBEAM R O
1 Bearsted Spot
Royal Electrical and Mechanical Engineers

PLUMMER FLORENCE (née Newsham)
Friningham Lodge
Women's Land Army

Florence married Marcus Radclyffe Plummer, Captain, Royal Engineers from Bere Regis, Dorset in 1945.

POCOCK TERENCE R
Aldworth, 212 Winifred Road
Royal Marines

POLLARD ERNEST F
3 Council Houses, The Street
Army

POUND DOUGLAS

POUND ------
Crest View, Hockers Lane
Royal Air Force

PRESCOTT-DENNIS WILLIAM F
173 Royston Road

PRICE HAROLD

PRINCE JOSEPH W T
St Albans, Plantation Lane

PURKESS JACK

RAGGETT CECIL M
Dilkoosha, Lord Romney's Hill

RAGGETT ERNEST EDWARD
Dilkoosha, Lord Romney's Hill
Single
Parents Mr and Mrs H Raggett
April 1938 Kent Civil Air Guard
Died 19 August 1939, aged 26

A transcript of the report from the Kent Messenger, 26 August 1939:

KENT CIVIL AIR GUARD PILOT KILLED

Nose Dive Caused By Attempt to Adjust Goggles?

Tragedy overtook an enthusiastic young airman, Civil Air Guard Pilot, Ernest Edward Raggett, son of Mr and Mrs H Raggett of Dilkoosha, Lord Romney's Hill, Maidstone, on Friday last week. As the plane he was flying passed over the playing field at Borough Green, at a low altitude, he was seen to wave frantically to the children below, evidently warning them to escape from danger. Then, almost immediately, the plane nose dived into an adjoining ploughed field. Witnesses of the crash rushed to the spot in order to render help, but they found the young airman, 26 years old, lifeless. He had, apparently been killed instantaneously.

MACHINE HALTED IN MID AIR

At the inquest at the Church Hall, Borough Green, on Tuesday, the suggestion was put forward by Mr G W Harrison, Chief Instructor for Maidstone and Malling Airdromes, that Mr Raggett might have been troubled by the fact that as he was taking off for the flight, which ended in the crash, his goggles fell off.

It might have been, said Mr Harrison, that he had flown on adjusting his goggles and did not know where he was. The inquest was conducted by Mr J H Soady (County Coroner) and a verdict of Accidental Death was returned. Sympathy was expressed by the jury and representatives of the airdrome with the relatives.

VERY KEEN ON FLYING

Herbert Edward Raggett identified his son, who, he said, lived with him and was a butcher with witness at Wrotham Heath.

His son as a member of the Civil Air Guard, which he joined last April. He was very keen on flying and was happy about the progress he was making. He was not at all nervous.

Dr Ralph Green, Borough Green, said that Mr Raggett had a fractured base of the skull and there were extensive injuries. Death would have been instantaneous.

Graham William Harrison, Hill View, Tonbridge Road, Teston, Chief Instructor for the Maidstone and Malling Airdromes said Mr Raggett was a pupil at his airdrome. He started training on April 19th. Up to August 16th he had had 11 hours 35 minutes dual flying and he then went up for a solo flight of ten minutes. He was flying very well. On Friday witness sent him up for half an hour's solo on practise landings.

MACHINE IN PROPER ORDER

The machine was in proper order and witness had been up in it with Mr Raggett previously on Friday evening.

When Mr Raggett took off, his goggles fell off and he rose erratically as he was trying to adjust them. This caused witness some concern and he watched for Mr Raggett to return.

EYE WITNESS STORY

George Henry Paul Greengarth, Ightham, said that on Friday evening he was in Borough Green Recreation Ground and about 7.30 saw a light airplane flying overhead at about 300-400 feet. The plane had flown from the direction of Malling and turned back. It made another turn, losing height and turned again, still dropping.

"I realised there was the possibility of a crash," said witness, "and at the time it stalled and crashed, I estimated it was about 120 feet up." The engine was operating the whole time and seemed to be functioning perfectly.

The machine seemed to halt in mid-air, its tail went up and it came crashing to earth. When he arrived at the scene of the crash he believed the goggles were on Mr Raggett's helmet. Police-Sgt Cooper, Borough Green, said the machine crashed on Whiffen's Farm. The nose was in the ground and the plane was completely smashed.

Reproduced courtesy of Kent Messenger group

This photograph of Red Cross, Kent 226 detachment, was taken in the garden of Bearsted House, home of Mr and Mrs Stanley Johnson, in 1944. They allowed part of their home to be used for many wartime organisations. It was the headquarters of the Home Guard and Air Raid Precautions, a distribution point for gas masks and a Red Cross centre. Training courses were regularly held there. The facilities even extended to a small hospital ward and Mr Johnson bought a small ambulance for the area.

Photograph courtesy of Jenni Hudson

Included in the photograph:

Back row:

Connie King; Eileen Blandford; Margery Foster

Second row:

Joyce Clark; Billie Hilton, Assistant Commandant; Mrs Bloggs, Commandant; Mrs Kemball; Peggy Sanders

Front row:

Sister Beeton Pull; Mrs Hollands; Mrs Wilkinson; Elsie Attwood; Sybil Mercer; Mildred Sierakowski; Mrs Jessel

Seated at front:

Mrs Stanley Johnson and Kath Kemball.

RANGE CHARLES D
Aldington Court Cottages
Army

RAVENSCROFT JAMES M E
Verman, Spot Lane

RAYMOND DUNCAN

RAYNER EUAN T
The Cottage, Thurnham Lane
Royal Army Ordnance Corps Warrant Officer

REATCHLOUS ANTONY
Knowle Cottage, The Green

REATCHLOUS RICHARD
Knowle Cottage, The Green

REEK RONALD G
Hamilton, The Grove

REES WILLIAM J
Amesbury, Spot Farm Estate
Royal Signals

REES ------
The Haven, Lord Romney's Hill
Royal Engineers

RELF MARISE JACQUELINE (née Humphreys)
Marise, Spot Lane
Women's Land Army

Marise married Robert Arthur Relf, Staff Sergeant, Royal Electrical and Mechanical Engineers of 58 Postley Road, Maidstone in 1945

REEVES FRANK E
Lunsford, Lord Romney's Hill

RING Mrs IRENE
7 Council Houses, The Street
Auxiliary Territorial Services

RING JOHN
7 Council Houses, The Street

ROBBINS ARTHUR S
Artily, 17 Spot Farm Estate

RUGG JOHN R
17 The Grove

RUSSELL GORDON B
Strutton House

RUSSELL JOHN S
Rostrevor, Ashford Road
Royal Navy

RUSSELL ROBERT *
Married
Wife Stella Rossetta Russell of Linton
Parents Adopted son of Conrad and Mabel Payne
Royal Navy H M S Hecla
Service Number C/MX 51149 Petty Officer Supply
Died 12 November 1942, aged 29
Commemorated 64; 1, Chatham Naval Memorial

SACKETT HAROLD G
Thornbank, Hockers Lane

SAGE LILIAN

SAGGERS WILLIAM F
50 Royston Road

SCOTT THOMAS R †
Thornham Friars
Married
Wife Yvonne Celeste Scott
Parents Frederick Robert and Ethel Mary Scott
Royal Air Force Volunteer Reserve
Service Number 962240 Sergeant
Died 30 October 1945, aged 28
Buried in grave 6254, section 18, Surbiton Cemetery, Surrey

SEDGE CHARLES
4 Council Houses, The Street

SEDGE EDITH (née Curtis)
4 Council Houses, The Street
Auxiliary Territorial Services

SELBY WILLIAM H
Fauchons House, Fauchons Lane
Royal Navy

SELVES HENRY

SENT J
Special Constable

SHARMAN WILLIAM H
Regina, Royston Road

SHARP ERNEST W
Tredene, Rosemary Road

SHAW HENRY J
Jesmond, Royston Road

SHERIFF FRANCIS

SHORTER EDWARD *+
The Street
Single
Parents Alfred Charles and Edith Lilian Shorter
4th Battalion, The Queen's Own (Royal West Kent Regiment)
Service Number 6346632 Private
Died 27 May 1940, aged 21
Buried in grave 6 A 3, Le Grand Hasard Military Cemetery, Morbecque, Nord, France

Edward was the sixth child of Alfred and Edith Shorter. This undated photograph shows Edward practising his salute:

Photograph courtesy of Rosemary Smith

SHORTER JACK
3 Chrisfield Cottages, The Green

SIMMONS D F
4 Egypt Place

SKINNER ROBERT
Harangor, Ashford Road
Royal Observer Corps, Bearsted

SMITH DAVID

SMITH ERNEST
Coronel, Royston Road

SMITH FRANKLIN W M

SMITH FREDERICK A W
Reneric, The Landway
Royal Air Force

SMITH LESLIE T
Winter Haven, Ashford Road

SMITH RONALD W
Thornbank, Weavering

SNOOK ANTHONY J
Bracondale, Plantation Lane
Royal Air Force

SPRINGETT CYRIL

SPRINGETT JAMES A
2 Holly Villas

SQUIRRELL STANLEY A
218 Winifred Road
Army

STARNES ALBERT F
205 Winifred Road

STILES WILLIAM H
The Old Water Tower, Tower Lane

STRINGER MAURICE W

STROUD JOHN H
Tuckenay, Spot Farm Estate

SUTTON CHARLES

SWAIN ARTHUR E D
193 Winifred Road

SWIFT ALBERT
4 Egypt Place

SWIFT DENNIS H
4 Egypt Place
Army

SWIFT FRANK
1 Council Cottages, Spot Lane

TANNER ALFRED H
Alflicot, Roseacre Lane
Royal Air Force

TAYLOR EDWARD

TAYLOR G KAY
Newlands, Tower Lane

TAYLOR J W
Fox Farm Cottages, Thurnham
Royal Navy

TAYLOR JAMES I
Glenlivet, Spot Lane

TAYLOR LESLIE J
South View, Ashford Road

TAYLOR ROSE M
Fox Farm Cottages, Thurnham
Auxiliary Territorial Services

TAYLOR WILLIAM
Fox Farm Cottages, Thurnham
Royal Electrical and Mechanical Engineers

TEBBUTT ANN
Moorings, Ashford Road

TEMPLE DAISY MURIEL (née Brown)
Court Farm, Thurnham
Navy Army and Air Force Institute

Daisy married Alan Temple, Royal Engineers, of Knaresborough, in 1945

TERRY DOUGLAS S
Church Farm, Ashford Road
Royal Artillery

TERRY FRANK S
Church Farm, Ashford Road
Gordon Highlanders

TERRY GORDON
10 Pine Grove
Army

THOMAS MAY I
Hill House, Ashford Road

THORPE MONICA A
Lilk Mount, Otham turning
Women's Auxiliary Air Force Aircraft Woman 2nd Class

THORPE PAMELA IANTHE
See entry for LAWRENCE

TILEY NORMAN F
Woodcroft, The Grove

TILL REGINALD L J
Oddicombe, The Grove

TINNING V M
Aldington Court Cottages
Auxiliary Territorial Service

TOLHURST ROY
3 West View, Roseacre Lane

TOLHURST WILLIAM
Newlyn, Yeoman Lane
Royal Army Service Corps

TONE SAMUEL

TOOMEY A

TRENCH CHRISTOPHER

TREVETT R J
Volage, Hockers Lane
Royal Navy

TROTT GEORGE
Rosemary, Spot Farm Estate

TUBB CHARLES

TUBB GEORGE E
Amberleigh, Yeoman Lane

TUBB JOHN

TURNER EDWARD G
The Laurels, Yeoman Lane

TUTT LIONEL N
The Nook, Weavering Street
Royal Air Force

TURRELL LESLIE W C
Sutton Street

USMAR ROBERT W
Walnut Tree Lodge, Weavering
Royal Air Force

VANE MOLLY
1 Oak Villas, The Green
Women's Auxiliary Air Force

VAUGHAN BETTY FRANCES (née Harrison)
Voluntary Aid Detachment, Bearsted House

Betty married Rowland Vaughan, Bombardier, of 42 Unity Street, Sittingbourne, in 1945

VAUGHAN REGINALD J
Drayton House, Spot Lane

VICKERS WILFRED
Orchard Lee, Ashford Road

VIDLER ARTHUR J B
Polperro, The Landway

VIDLER JOHN

WALKER RONALD H
Golf View, Ware Street

WALKLING B
Special Constable

WALTERS JOHN H
7 Council Houses, The Street

WARLAND ALAN

WATCHAM WALTER S
Vicarage Cottages, Church Lane

WATERS LESLIE

WATKINS LESLIE
Golf View, Ware Street

WATSON JOAN F
Quilter's Cottage, Otham turning

WATSON JOHN

WEAVER RONALD
The Royal Oak

WELFARE DESMOND

WELLER A
3 Egypt Place, The Street
Army

WELLS SIDNEY J
Spot Farm

WHITE CHARLES D
Denby, Fauchons Lane

WHITE GRAHAM W
Little Dane, Thurnham

WHITE HERBERT LIONEL *+
Single
Parents George and Ellen (née Chapman) White
Royal Army Service Corps
Service Number T/84868 Driver
Died 30 May 1940, aged 20
Note: Bearsted war memorial date is 31 May 1940

Herbert was born 2 January 1920 at Manor Farm, Bredhurst. He was the eighth child and sixth son. He was baptized at St Peter's, Bredhurst on 25 May 1920. The family moved to The Harrow public house, Lidsing, until 1928. George was the tenant at Madginford Farm in the 1930s. The farm was a fruit tree nursery. Later, some of the land became the site of the Madginford schools.

Herbert attended Bearsted School and Holy Cross Sunday School. All his family: grandmothers, great aunts and brothers lived in Bearsted. Herbert left school in 1935. By 1939 he was a cold store engineer and a member of the Territorial Army. He was called up with two brothers in 1939 and served in the British Expeditionary Force in Belgium, driving large supply lorries.

He re-enlisted in the Royal Army Service Corps. It is believed that Herbert embarked on a ship which was torpedoed or blown up on 29 – 30 May 1940. His parents thought he was a prisoner of war until his water-damaged belongings were returned to them. An inscription to Herbert is to be found on his brother, Horace's grave in Holy Cross churchyard, Bearsted.

WHITE JACK C
Denby, Fauchons Lane

WHITE LESLIE A
Denby, Fauchons Lane
Royal Army Service Corps

WHITE PERCY
Denby, Fauchons Lane

WHITE PHILIP B
The Cottage, Thurnham Lane

WHITEHEAD CHARLES

This cartoon depicting a cricket match between The Hon Tennyson's Eleven and Mr Plum Warner's Eleven was drawn by Eric Green in 1942. The two teams were described as those 'Under 40' and those 'Over 40'. The cartoon includes many people from Bearsted and Thurnham:

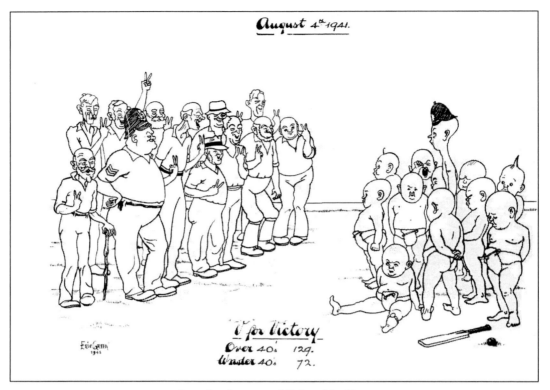

August 4th 1941.

V for Victory
Over 40's 129.
Under 40's 72.

Reproduced courtesy of Chris and Sue Hunt

WICKS WARDEN ARTHUR †*
The Queen's Own (Royal West Kent Regiment)
Attached to 13th (Labour) Battalion, Queen's (Royal West Surrey Regiment)
Service Number 14858994 Private
Died 8 March 1945
Buried in grave 904, New Churchyard (situated at Lower Green), St Peter's church, Pembury

WIDDOWSON VINCENT
Willington Road
Royal Air Force

WILKINSON GEORGE

WILLIAMS A
Oakedeane, Firs Lane, Ashford Road
Royal Artillery

WILLIAMS ALFRED L
5 Pine Grove

WILLIAMS G T
1 May's Cottages, Ware Street
Royal Engineers

WILLIAMS HENRY J
Little Orchard, Royston Road

WILSON ALBERT E
Winton, Fauchons Lane

WILSON ROBERT

WILSON THOMAS

WISE J

WOOD HERBERT C
Holmbury, Royston Road
Royal Corps of Signals

WORLEY PHILIP G
163 Royston Road

WORTH DONALD
165 Royston Road
Royal Air Force

WRAIGHT H J
The Queen's Own (Royal West Kent Regiment)
Service Number 6096089 Sergeant

WYE ANTHONY V P
Old Tiles, Roundwell

WYNDHAM-GREEN G A
1 Roseacre Terrace, Tower Lane
Royal Army Service Corps

YUILL RONALD
Renfrew, Cavendish Way

ZEE REGINALD

Many men in Bearsted and Thurnham that did not serve in the armed forces, volunteered to join the Bearsted branch of the Royal Observer Corps. Their lookout post was located on Mr Bradley's land, which is now part of The Landway. This undated photograph shows some of the members:

Photograph courtesy of Evelyn Pearce

Included in the photograph:

Back row:

L Monckton; B Abel; F Harnett

Middle row:

F Grout; B Moss; Mr McLonegal; Mr Cooper; N Dearing

Front row:

Robert Skinner

To mark Victory in Europe in 1945, many local celebrations were held. This photograph was taken next to the unlit bonfire built in Shirley Way and includes Len Mercer, Mr Fairbrass, Herbert Coales, Henry Hadley, Mr Rayner-Sharp, James Strettle, Mr Passmore and John Coales.

Photograph courtesy of Edith Coales

Memories of the Second World War

Doris Britcher, neé Bentley, moved to Bearsted in October 1935 from Liverpool. These are some of her memories about her life during the war.

I was about twelve years old when war broke out. My teacher at Bearsted School was Miss Horsman. She lived with her mother in a house near Yeoman shops and we all knew that her father was German. I remember that before the war, she was always keen to hurry her class home at the end of the day as she liked to listen to the German programme broadcast on the wireless at 4pm, two to three times a week. She was an excellent teacher, kind but firm to her class and had no favourites. However, as the international situation worsened, there were suspicions in the village that her loyalty was elsewhere. We all knew that she had a German boyfriend who was a member of the Nazi party.

A few months before war was declared, she selected the ten best writers in the class to write some letters to a German boys school. The idea was that there would then be a correspondence between the schools. Miss Horsman gave us some ideas to put in our letters: I clearly recall that I thought it was rather strange when she said that the information that she would like to see included was that Bearsted was just over a mile away from an airfield at Detling, the school had a railway line running along one side of the boundary, the cathedral city of Canterbury was only twenty or so miles away and could be easily reached by train, the nearest town was Maidstone which was just over two miles away and regularly had soldiers stationed there. However, all of this information had to be mixed with descriptions of some of the children's other activities such as Guides and the King's Messengers (this was a church group in the village that supported the work of missionaries such as Grace Dibble).

I eventually received a reply from a boy called Willi Wintermere. Parts of the letter seemed strange though. He included the information that he went to a Youth Group which was similar to the Boy Scouts but was called the "German Youth Movement". After war was declared, I was rather worried about the letter so I destroyed it. I do sometimes wonder what happened to Willi Wintermere. Miss Horsman stayed on at the school but I think that Robert Skinner was aware where her sympathies lay and she eventually left. I am not entirely sure if she was interned.

Until the summer of 1939, everything seemed to be quite normal to nearly everyone in the village. However, once war was declared, the school did not properly re-open until October 1939 as the evacuees from Plumstead School arrived. Extra classrooms had to be used in the village including the Clock Room of the Men's Institute, the Methodist Chapel, the Women's Institute and the Mission Room in Ware Street. Half-days of school were arranged but there was very little joint teaching with the London school. The headmaster of the Plumstead School lived in Yeoman Way with his family.

I remember the August day in 1940 that Detling airfield was bombed very clearly indeed. We had decided to have a family picnic on the Green that day. We played lots of games and had spread a blanket on the grass. We had just started to eat our sandwiches when a terrific roaring sound approached from the direction of the church (it certainly didn't sound like Spitfire or Lancaster air planes) came over the Green and straight over our heads just as the Air Raid siren sounded. It was unusual for an attack to take place on a cloudy day as we had heard that the German pilots preferred to see the ground that they intended to bomb. Somehow the planes had avoided the radar system: the air was black with them. We later estimated that there had been around forty planes.

We were terrified and threw everything into the baby's pram whilst we tried to think where we could shelter as there did not seem to be anyone else around. Almost miraculously, Mrs Pellet appeared at the front door of her house, which was near the Men's Institute, and frantically beckoned us to come in. We stayed at her house for hours whilst the raid took place at the airfield. The sound of the raid carried straight over the hills from Detling and we could hear it so clearly.

During the raid, I tried so hard not to think of where my father was and not to worry, but it was quite impossible. He was based at Detling and working as a clerk for a construction company. Finally, I saw him approaching on a bicycle passing by the pond on the Green. He had managed to escape the bombing but was deeply shocked. A neighbour, Mrs Munn, had advised him of the whereabouts of his family.

This photograph shows Bearsted School in 1943. Note that the foundation stone, located over the top of the central window on the left hand side of the building, has been covered with a fine wire netting:

Photograph courtesy of Roseacre School

Mr Skinner was always very careful about children whose relatives were killed or posted as "Missing" in the war. On one occasion, I remember that he sent Betty Gibbens on an errand and used the time to tell the children that a boat had been sunk and it looked as if her father had been lost with the rest of the crew.

The Hodges family that lived at Rosemount Dairy farm had a near miss one night, when a bomb lodged on a nearby railway embankment. Robert Skinner's look of relief when Jean walked into school the next day said so much about the way he cared for all of his pupils.

Robert Skinner looked after us extremely well during the war years. It could not have been easy for him having to cope with the extra children that had been evacuated from Plumstead, but he was determined that we would be fully prepared for every eventuality.

I think that my generation certainly owes an immense debt to Robert Skinner, and to the older generations in Bearsted and Thurnham that had already lived through the First World War. Although they now had another war to cope with, the outstanding care and examples of courage that they displayed every day helped the younger people to meet the difficulties and shortages that occurred.

This photograph was taken as the evacuees from Plumstead arrived at Bearsted:

Photograph courtesy of Jessie Page

During the Second World War, many women went out to work; some of them for the first time. Women filled gaps in the workforce that were left by men who were serving in the armed forces. In December 1941, the Government called up unmarried women between 20 and 30 years of age to serve in the auxiliary forces: Auxiliary Territorial Services, Women's Royal Naval Service, Women's Army Auxiliary Corps and the Women's Auxiliary Air Force. Women were employed as mechanics, radio operators or ambulance drivers.

Joan Harden (née Margetts) joined the ATS. She began her service career in 1942 working on anti-aircraft and searchlight batteries and ended the war as a corporal. Joan recalled that when the radar showed enemy aircraft approaching, her team was immediately deployed. At first, the ATS girls acted primarily as height and range-finders. German bombers would be located and then the exact position was plotted so that the guns would be on target. These calculations were done by machine and passed onto the team in control of the guns. At the order, 'on target, fire', the guns opened up with a deafening roar and the ground shook beneath their feet.

At the end of 1940, the pressing shortage of numbers forced the authorities to give women a wider role in the armed forces. By August 1941, the first anti-aircraft battery to include both men and women was deployed in Richmond Park. They became the first women to take a combatant role in any army in the world.

Joan was sent to France after the country was liberated in 1944 and became part of the team manning the anti-aircraft gun defences along the channel coast. She assisted in the controlled use of barrage balloons. The discipline was strict: they were not allowed out of their quarters at night and a strict curfew was enforced. Despite the privations, the dangers and the routine fourteen mile marches that were part of her training, Joan thoroughly enjoyed every minute of her time in the forces. It was not all hard work and the social side of army life was great fun.

Rest, relaxation and recuperation for the armed forces

During the war, leisure pursuits for members of the armed forces stationed nearby, largely involved participating in activities and events in Bearsted and Thurnham. These were held in at many different venues including the function room at The White Horse, the Memorial Hall, the Tudor House and the Women's Institute. At the latter, dances and concerts were organised by the Entertainments National Service Association. Further afield, the Star Ballroom in Maidstone was also a regular venue, particularly as men in uniform were charged a lower admittance fee, or occasionally, there was no charge.

In Bearsted, the Royal Oak, was used by soldiers from New Zealand that were stationed in Bearsted Cottage and Mote Park. It was known that the soldiers were quite generous with their rations, which seemed to be ample in comparison to British allowances. Corned beef sandwiches were nearly always available at the pub, so it was assumed that some of the military catering supplies had found their way to the Royal Oak! This undated photograph shows part of the Royal Oak building and the main entrance:

Photograph courtesy of Terry Clark

It did not take long for The White Horse to become part of the circuit of public houses visited by airmen from Detling aerodrome. They included sergeants from Thurnham Court, and their officers based at Thornham Friars and Cobham Manor.

Roger Vidler was able to discover from older residents of Bearsted and Thurnham that many of the armed forces from the area were attracted to the regular dance nights held at the White Horse. Among those to attend were Canadian troops stationed at Vinters Park. The dances were held in a function room which had been added to the White Horse in Victorian times. The venue later became part of the Beefeater restaurant. Sometimes, over a hundred people would cram in to the confined space, waltzing, fox-trotting and jitter-bugging the night away to the sounds of an army band.

The dances were very popular but the armed forces were not known for their dancing skills. It did not take long for the events to be referred to as 'football matches'. The events were hugely attractive to the young people of the village, but it is debatable whether the presence of some mothers acting as chaperones were regarded in a similar light! The dances continued throughout the war and were never once stopped by an air raid.

The landlady, Mrs Benjamin Brook, who was known to everyone as 'Auntie Ben', kept a special panel in one of the bars for the airmen to sign their names. In subsequent redecorations, she refused to have the panel painted over. This undated photograph of the White Horse gives some indication of the appearance of the pub. The building on the right hand side of the photograph was a stable block:

Photograph courtesy of Roger Vidler

The Black Horse at Thurnham was one of the nearest public houses for the men stationed at Detling aerodrome. This undated photograph of the Black Horse gives an indication of the appearance of the pub:

Photograph courtesy of Martin Elms

Thurnham Keep, Thurnham Court and the former vicarage of St Mary's, Thurnham were requisitioned for armed forces accommodation as they were close to Detling aerodrome. Thurnham Keep became a convalescence home for wounded aircrew from Detling aerodrome. The building dates from 1910 and it is believed that the flint wall dressing came from the ruins of Thurnham Castle. The fittings in the house were of a superb quality and included wooden panelling and marble. This recent photograph shows the outside of the house:

Photograph courtesy of Roger Vidler

The cellars of the house were used to store important and highly confidential Air Ministry documents. An escape route also had to be devised for use in the event of the house being bombed so that personnel and documents could be safely removed. A short tunnel was excavated which led from the cellars into woodland in the North Downs which are behind the house. Fortunately, use of the tunnel was never required. It has now been blocked off at the far end. This photograph shows part of the tunnel today:

Photograph courtesy of Roger Vidler

At the former vicarage, a bar for Royal Air Force officers, was located in a ground floor room. Some redecoration of the rooms was undertaken, largely in shades of yellow, green and brown. It is thought that during this time, the bar area was decorated by an air force regiment with a series of wall paintings undertaken in aircraft paint. This photograph of the former vicarage was taken in the early years of the Twentieth century:

Photograph courtesy of Michael Perring

After the war, in 1946, the house was sold to Mr and Mrs White. Evelyn Fridd and Margaret Plowright (née White) recalled that their parents renamed the house Little Dane as the Church Commissioners who sold it insisted that the property should not bear a name that had any ecclesiastical connection. Although the building needed a thorough renovation, Mr White was a builder, and so he was able to undertake the work. The house was later sold to Mr and Mrs Ashdown who uncovered the wall paintings in 1998. In the process of further restoration and modernisation, they have also found other artefacts such as some Royal Air Force signs in the cellar. These photographs show details from two of the wall paintings:

Photographs courtesy of Downs Mail

The Second World War for the Palmer family

The Palmer family came to Bearsted when their home in London was bombed in 1940. There were six children: Rose, Mary, Joan, Ann, Edward and Joyce. Their parents had met shortly after the First World War, whilst hop-picking in Caring Lane, so the family knew the area very well. They lived in Manor Rise before moving to Shirley Way in 1942.

Mr Palmer had been severely injured in the First World War. His injuries had left him physically quite weak and regarded as completely disabled; at the age of eighteen and a half. Four years before the Second World War started, Mr Palmer had been advised by a doctor that he was still so physically frail that if he continued to work, he would not see his fortieth birthday. He therefore spent a great deal of his time looking after the family whilst his wife went out to work.

When war was declared, Ann and Joan were evacuated with their school to Somerset. Many of their classmates swiftly returned to London. Instead, Ann and Joan joined their family in Bearsted and for a short time attended Bearsted School before leaving in 1943.

Normal life during the war was difficult. Food rationing was a challenge with a large family to feed, but they were all continually amazed at the way Mrs Palmer managed to produce meals for them. They were registered as customers of the Co-operative store at the Yeoman area of Bearsted. Mary always regarded dried egg as tasting unpleasant but Spam was completely unpalatable, despite her mother's best efforts to disguise it in batter!

One of Joan's first jobs was working in a dress shop, or 'gown shop' as it was known, in Week Street. She recalled that there was a cellar under the shop and it was rumoured that a river ran below the premise. The shop had very little stock due to the ration restrictions and the introduction of clothing coupons. Clothes from wholesale stockists could only be obtained through coupons, redeemed from customers. As there was very little in the shop to sell, it was difficult to produce these and prove to wholesalers that there was a demand. One day, Joan and another colleague decided to see if there was anything in the cellar that they could bring into use for stock, as the shop was looking very bare. They found a chest of drawers in a corner but it could not be easily opened due to the damp atmosphere. Eventually, they prised the drawers open and discovered many items, including taffeta bridesmaids dresses, which had been put away, seemingly 'for the duration'. They made up a window display with some of the clothes. Their pride in their resourcefulness was short-lived however, as a passer-by was heard referring to the shop as selling stock which appeared to be 'what came out before the ark'!

If clothing was difficult to obtain, new shoes were almost impossible to find at times, even if enough points were accumulated. Joan and Mary decided to wear clogs for while and so spare extra wear and tear on their shoes. They were rather surprised to find that the clogs had wooden soles and were studded with hobnails. It did not take them long to discover that it was difficult to walk any distance wearing them as they were just too uncomfortable. Also, if the wood splintered or was rough, there was a good chance of a ladder or hole appearing in a very precious pair of stockings.

During the war, Edward Palmer became eligible to be called up for service in either the armed forces or other war work. Freddie Grout, who owned Yeoman Garage, offered to employ Edward in his machine shop. The garage's usual business of supplying petrol was limited due to restrictions and rationing, so Freddie took on different contracts which assisted the war effort and employed local people. The garage employees finished aircraft parts. It was known locally that Freddie Grout clearly regarded it as his patriotic duty to employ people on this sort of work. The majority of the contracts involved assembling parts for planes which were delivered in packs in a rough state. They were then prepared, drilled and tapped, machined and assembled.

Despite all the restrictions imposed through rationing, Joan recalled that one of the very worst aspects about the war was the bombing of the towns and cities. The very hostility of bombing, that people could inflict such horrific damage on each other, was a major shock. Mary remembered that after the first night of bombing in England when the London docks were attacked by the Luftwaffe, the blaze was clearly visible from Wrotham Hill as she travelled there on a bus. The journey came to an abrupt end when they reached the High Street at New Cross. Mary could clearly recall the bus coming to a halt by some two-storey shops as the air raid siren sounded. She was advised to head for a shelter of some sort as it would not be long before the German airplanes would be overhead. All the passengers took shelter at one end of a nearby school building.

The raid continued for many hours. When Mary emerged after the all clear signal sounded, she found the scene was reminiscent of Dante's Inferno. The two storey shops were all destroyed. The air was permeated with a smell which was a mixture of cordite, smoke and gas. Nothing was clearly visible as dust hung in the air like fog. The smell of gas came from a broken mains pipe in the wrecked road and small fires, which had not been wholly extinguished, lingered in areas that were blocked with shattered fragments of buildings. She was extremely lucky; the opposite end of the school in which she had sheltered had also been bombed and partially destroyed.

Mary could also vividly remember the bombing of Mill Street in Maidstone which took place in October 1940. At this time, Mary was working in Stonham chemists in Bank Street, Maidstone. Fairly early one morning, she caught a bus from Bearsted and was on the way into work when her bus passed a bus stop in the Sittingbourne Road. It was crowded with airmen who were waiting there for transport to Detling. As they went past, Mary noticed that all the men were looking up, watching as a stick of bombs fell from a German plane. The airmen suddenly dropped onto the ground as they realised what was going to happen and tried to take cover. The bus stopped and Mary went no further. Once again, she was immensely lucky; the back of the chemists premises was destroyed in the subsequent bomb blast in Mill Street.

When Victory in Europe was announced, for some time it seemed rather unreal that there was going to be no more bombing and destruction. However, it did not take long for the people living in Shirley Way to organise some celebrations. A massive bonfire was built on the roundabout in the road. Doris Britcher and Joyce Bourne (née Palmer) recalled that Mr Grout arranged a marvellous sports day to celebrate the ending of the war. Cavendish Way was used as the sports ground and a starting pistol was unearthed so that the events could be started correctly. Hilda, Muriel and Rita, sisters to Doris, all participated in the races. Hilda was a gifted athlete and won so many of the races that Mr Grout asked her to stand down from some of the events in order to give the other children a chance! The prizes were books of savings stamps.

For many people, although rationing would persist and there were continued difficulties in everyday life to overcome, for now, it was enough that the immediate war was over. For the first time in six years, people could dare to contemplate a future and have the luxury of being able to make plans.

Welcome Home: Second World War

After the end of the war, Bearsted and Thurnham parish councils decided to establish a committee to investigate ideas for an official Welcome Home celebration for everyone serving in the armed forces. On 12 November 1945 the committee agreed that souvenir scrolls would be presented and a dinner or concert held, if funds allowed. Recipients would be any man or woman who served in the forces between 1939 and 1945, having joined up before Victory over Japan Day, and included all the Merchant Services.[1]

In order to establish a list of those who were eligible, the committee members checked a card index held at the Bearsted branch of the British Legion, the Services Voting Register, subscriptions lists for the parish magazine and records held by the Red Cross. It was found that far more people than they had originally envisaged were eligible so a target of £500 was established. It is not clear whether this target was actually reached, but it was quickly agreed that if there were any surplus funds, they would be passed onto the British Legion.[2] Collection tins were distributed and posters were printed. Below is shown one of the posters:[3]

BEARSTED & THURNHAM
FORCES
WELCOME HOME
FUND

President : Mr. W. H. WHITEHEAD.

Hon. Treasurer: Mr. A. BARKER, Little Snowfield, Bearsted

Committee : Mrs. Markwick, Miss Sage, Rev. W. H. Yeandle, Messrs. L. R. S. Monckton. R. Skinner, E. A. Abery, W. B. Barnes, H. Humphrey, F. W. Grout, R. L. Lord, J. Flood, A. S. Perrin, Hon. Sec.

£500 WANTED

to welcome the men and women of the two parishes (over 300 in number) who have served in H.M. Forces.

Your help is invited.

Contributions, small or large, will be gratefully received by any of the above.

Reproduced courtesy of Centre for Kentish Studies

In order to accommodate the number of people expected to attend, it was arranged to hold two separate concerts in September 1946 and October 1947. Below is shown a card and letter of invitation:[4]

Subscribers to the
Bearsted & Thurnham Forces Welcome Home
Fund
request the pleasure of the company of

at a
Smoking Concert
to be held at the
Women's Institute, on Saturday, 2 8 SEP 1946,
at 7 p.m.
R.S.V.P   PLEASE PRESENT THIS CARD AT THE DOOR.

BEARSTED & THURNHAM FORCES WELCOME HOME FUND.

Hon. Sec. A. S. Perrin,
"Wendings,"
Roseacre Lane,
BEARSTED

Dear

The people of Bearsted and Thurnham, who have subscribed to the above Fund, extend a most hearty welcome to you to attend the first of a series of Smoking Concerts, arranged for Saturday, 2 8 SEP 1946, at the Women's Institute. As admission will be by card only, you are requested to present the enclosed official invitation card upon arrival.

This informal gathering is being held to welcome you back amongst your friends and to mark their appreciation of your past services. A most attractive programme of entertainment by Miss Colleen Clifford and her party of Radio and Television Artists has been arranged; there will be a buffet supper with both beer and soft drinks, in fact the whole evening is being organised in that spirit of happy informality which they feel would be your wish.

Please come along if you possibly can, and in order to help the ladies who have kindly undertaken the very difficult job of catering, will you please complete and post the enclosed postcard to reach me by September 15th, at the latest. You will appreciate how essential it is that the number attending should be known in good time.

Yours truly,

A S Perrin

Hon. Secretary,
Bearsted and Thurnham Forces Welcome Home Fund.

2nd September, 1946.

Reproduced courtesy of Centre for Kentish Studies

This is one of the commemorative certificates presented at the concerts:

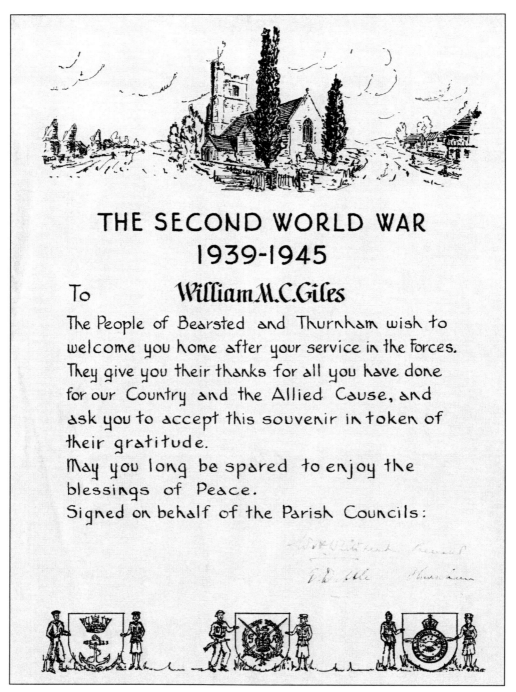

Reproduced courtesy of Norah Giles

War memorials in Bearsted and Thurnham

During the First World War, the Chairman of Bearsted Parish Council asked for names of all serving members in the community to be noted so that a Roll of Honour might be kept. Although the records have not survived, it is likely that Thurnham Parish Council also kept a similar list. Early in 1916, a public meeting was held in Bearsted to discuss the matter of a war memorial, but nothing appears to have been decided before the end of the war.

After the armistice, a war memorial committee for Bearsted was formed[1] under the Chairmanship of General Whitacre Allen. He was assisted by Mr Jones and Mr Tasker, together with Mr Harman, Mr Watts and Mr Charles Wilkinson. Plans were drawn up by Mr W D Caroë. Construction was undertaken by Messrs Corben and Son of Maidstone and the masons were Mr W H Kirk, Mr A Grayland, Mr H Palmer, Mr W Bowyer and Mr H Holloway. The cost was covered by the funds raised; around £270. The memorial was unveiled and dedicated 31 October 1919. Below is a partial transcript of the very full report from the Kent Messenger, 1 November 1919:

Memorial Cross Dedicated

Full of exquisite beauty and great solemnity was the service at the Church of the Holy Cross, Bearsted, on Thursday afternoon in commemoration of the villagers who have fallen in the war, and for the dedication of the memorial cross erected in the churchyard.

The business premises in the village were closed during the service; the flag of St George flew from the church tower at half mast, whilst a half muffled peal was rung on the bells. The chantry was reserved for relatives of the fallen, and the nave was reserved for some 60 men and women who had seen service with the colours. Not only was the church crowded, but many were unable to obtain admission. Amongst those present were Colonel, Mrs and Miss Lushington, Major MacQueen, Mr and Mrs W T Fremlin, Mrs H V Lushington, Mr and Mrs H Monckton, Mrs F D E Harnett, Mrs S Lance Monckton, Mr J Hampson, Mr H J Brook, Messrs T Ovenden, T H Bates, W H Smith, W T Paramor, G Hepden and Mitchell (representing the Wesleyan Church).

Immediately before the service commenced, Miss H R Hoar, the organist, played the Dead March in 'Saul', the congregation meanwhile standing. Then came the processional hymns 'Those whose course on earth is o'er.' Amongst those in the procession were the Bishop of Croydon, the Rural Dean (the Rev T G Lushington), the Revs F L Blamire Brown (Vicar), Canon E H Hardcastle, C Stonehouse, P Lambert, H P Brewer (Maidstone), Canon Horsley (Detling), H R Hughes (Leeds), W Gardner-Waterman (Loose), E H Jones (Hollingbourne), A Ogle (Otham), E H Lord (Sutton Valence), B T Milton (Boughton Monchelsea), T Chapman (Langley), H de V Watson (Harrietsham), Lieut-Colonel O J Daniell

and Mr H Watts (churchwardens), General Whitacre Allen, C B, the Revs S E Keeble (Wesleyan Minister), Messrs H Tasker, H V Lushington, W H Whitehead, O Jones, J Harman, C Wilkinson, A S Perrin, H Bensted, W Prime Jones, Spencer, J Corben, Lance Monckton, jun., J Hillier French, Supt Mepsted, Sergt Martin and P C Wellard.

The Vicar conducted the service, which included the hymns, 'Now the labourer's task is o'er', and 'O what joy,' and the Rural Dean read the lesson. At the close of the prayers the Last Post was sounded as the congregation stood in silence. From the chancel steps, the Bishop delivered an eloquent address…The choir and clergy, with the processional crosses and banners, and followed by the congregation, then proceeded to the churchyard, where the cross had been erected. Mr W H Whitehead, Chairman of the Parish Council, then presented to the Bishop the petition requesting him to dedicate the memorial, which he did, committing it to the care of the Vicar and Churchwardens. The hymns 'When I Survey the Wondrous Cross', 'The Cross, The Cross,' and the Te Deum were sung during the dedication, and the Reveille sounded. At the close of the service the flag was hoisted to the top of the mast and a peal was rung on the bells.

The cross, which stands 24 feet high, has a base of five tiers and is worked in Clipsham stone. The inscription reads: 'In thankful remembrance of the Cross of Christ and of the men of Bearsted, who laid down their lives for the brethren 1914-1919.' The names of the 25 men who fell are inscribed in panels…The stewards at the service were Messrs Corps, Brook, Goodman, Pressland, Stringer, Tullett and Beeston.

Reproduced courtesy of Kent Messenger group

St Mary's church, Thurnham, has several memorials to the First World War: a framed Roll of Honour, a stained glass window and an engraved brass plaque. The window and plaque were dedicated on 5 June 1920. Below is a photograph of the window and a transcript of the report from the Kent Messenger:

Photograph courtesy of Roger Vidler

THURNHAM'S WAR MEMORIAL

Stained Glass Window Dedicated

On Monday evening, Thurnham Church was crowded on occasion of the dedication of a handsome stained glass memorial window in honour of the nineteen Thurnham heroes who made the grand sacrifice in the Great War. The service, which was characterised by much impressiveness, commenced with the processional choir being followed up the aisle by the Rev F J Blamire Brown (Bearsted), S R Wigan (vicar) and the Bishop of Dover. Colonel A Wood Martyn unveiled the window, which was dedicated by the Bishop, who read the names of the men.

After the singing of "For all the saints, who from their labours rest", the Bishop preached from the text "Greater love hath no man than this: that a man lay down his life for his friends". He reminded those who had lost loved ones that with their natural sorrow must come a feeling of reverent pride at the thought that it was through their hopes, and brothers,

and others like them, in all parts of the country that our land today was safe by God's mercy. It was fitting that those who had bravely given of their lives should never be forgotten, and the memorial window would through generations be the beautiful reminder of what the brave lads of Thurnham did in the Great War. The concluding hymn was 'O God, our help in ages past', and the National Anthem was also sung. Mr Gardner presided at the organ and at the conclusion, impressively played the Dead March.

The memorial window, which is on the south side of the church, is a beautiful representation of St Michael and St George – executed by Messrs Heaton, Butler and Rayne, of Garrick Street, London. Below the window, upon a brass tablet, are the names of the men, engraved by Mr R C Godden, of Maidstone.

Reproduced courtesy of Kent Messenger group

After the Second World War, Thurnham parish council arranged for a wooden memorial plaque to be placed in St Mary's church, recording the names of those who died in the war. A Roll of Honour was also framed and hung in the porch of the church. Below is shown the wooden plaque:

TO THE MEMORY OF THE MEN
OF THURNHAM PARISH WHO
DIED IN THE WAR 1939 – 1945
CHARLES H.D. FROST
WALTER COOKSON   JOHN A. GILBERT
ROBERT G. GUEST   THOMAS HARRISON
JESSE G. HUNT   FREDERICK LOCKYER
JOHN C. MACIVER   REGINALD PENNEY
THOMAS R. SCOTT   WARDEN A. WICKS

Photograph courtesy of Roger Vidler

Bearsted parish council decided to record the names of their casualties by adding them to the memorial for the First World War. An extra layer of stone was therefore added to each step on the memorial, as shown in the picture of the memorial below. The work was undertaken by Messrs Witcombe and Son of Maidstone.

Photograph courtesy of Malcolm Kersey

After the alterations, the memorial was unveiled and re-dedicated in a service held in Bearsted churchyard on 17 June 1947. The following special prayer was used:

In the Faith of Jesus Christ, we re-dedicate this Cross to the Glory of God and in memory of those who gave their lives in the Two World Wars for Freedom, in the Name of the Father, and of the Son, and of the Holy Ghost. *Amen*

Reproduced courtesy of Jenni Hudson

The inscription was unveiled by Mr Thomas R Lee, late Company Quarter Master Sergeant of the 2nd Battalion, Royal Warwickshire Regiment, who had been held as a prisoner of war in Germany from 1940 to 1945. Wreaths were laid by Mr A H Holtum and Mr E A Abery on behalf of the Bearsted and Thurnham branch of the British Legion.

This is the front of service booklet:

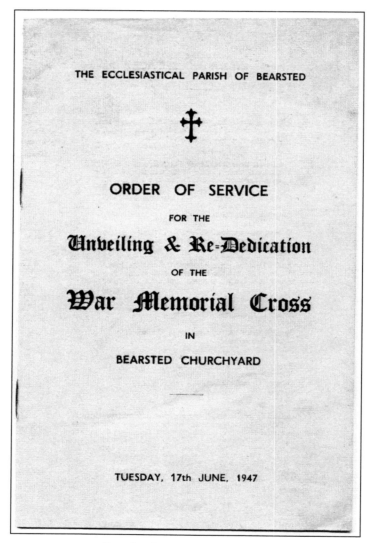

Reproduced courtesy of Jenni Hudson

Holy Cross church also has a memorial stained glass window that is dedicated to the memory of William Hugh Parkin and the crew of H M S Glorious. The window replaced one of Victorian design that had been badly damaged by bomb blasts during the war. The church authorities took the opportunity that the installation of the new window provided to make a number of changes to the building. On either side of the east window, and on the north and south sides of the sanctuary, were six paintings of saints. Below these were panels of coloured tiling. Permission was given for all the decoration to be removed. It was hoped that by simplifying the setting, the window could be given greater prominence. The pictures of the saints were carefully reframed and hung elsewhere in the church.

The new window was commissioned by the Whitehead family and designed by Mr Francis H Spear, ARCA, FRSA, of Stanmore, Middlesex. He was an artist in stained glass who made his own materials in his studio. The theme of the new window was the Lord in Glory.

In the photograph below can be seen the finished window. The centre light shows Christ seated on the Throne of Glory, with the earth as His footstool. In the tracery above are the emblems of Christ's passion. The left and right hand lights contain images of the patron saints of the armed forces. On the left is Saint George, wearing armour and holding a palm branch; emblematic of martyrdom. Below him is Saint Nicholas, the patron saint of sailors. He is holding a representation of H M S Glorious.

Photograph courtesy of Roger Vidler

167

In the right hand light is St Michael, 'Captain of the Hosts of the Lord', holding a flaming sword outstretched. He became, by common consent, the patron saint of the Royal Air Force. Above him is Saint Stephen. He is emblematic of Civil Defence workers and all others, not in the three main armed services, but who lost their lives in the war. At the foot of the left hand light are the arms and crest of the Parkin family. Slightly above them is the crest of H M S Glorious; a Tudor rose, from which emerges rays of gold and silver.

At the foot of the right hand light are the arms of the See of Canterbury and the County of Kent. The inscription reads:

> May the Lord in Glory mercifully receive William Hugh Parkin and those aboard H M S Glorious who perished with him, and all others from Bearsted and elsewhere, who died that we may live.

The photograph below shows the detail of Saint Nicholas:

Photograph courtesy of Roger Vidler

On 18 January 1948, on his thirteenth birthday, William Hugh Parkin unveiled the window that was dedicated to his father and the 1,200 other members of the crew that had also died. The service was conducted by the Vicar of Bearsted and the dedication was made by the Bishop of Dover, the Right Rev A C W Rose. The Bishop also preached on the Communion of Saints.

Robert Skinner, Headmaster of Bearsted School, recorded the names of the five Old Scholars who were killed in the war on a memorial sundial. It was erected at the front of the school and on 27 July 1949, the sundial was dedicated by the Bishop of Dover. Although Mr Skinner had hoped to obtain a printed copy of an order of service, there was not time. Instead there was a duplicated typed sheet in which he advised that that he hoped to prepare a printed leaflet about the memorial in due course.[2]

Below is a transcript of the service sheet:

A prayer for the school

A prayer of thanks for the school founders and benefactors

A prayer of General Thanksgiving

Psalm 23 (sung by the school)

The Dedication of the Sundial by the Rt Rev, the Bishop of Dover

A prayer for the fallen

The Lord's Prayer

Hymn 128 from The Children's Hymn Book: *Land of our Birth*
(words by Rudyard Kipling, tune: *Psalmodia Evangelica* 1790)

The National Anthem (verses 1-3)

Reproduced courtesy of Edith Coales

This photograph accompanied a report in the Kent Messenger newspaper about the service:

Photograph courtesy of Kent Messenger Group

The children marked Armistice Day later that year by laying a wreath at the sundial and thereby began a tradition at the school for every Remembrance Day. When the school re-located to new premises at The Landway in 1972, the sundial was also moved. Although the memorial is now in a different setting, the central courtyard of the school, a Remembrance Service continues to be held in recognition of the sacrifice made by the Old Scholars.[3]

Appendix 1
Battle of Britain casualties

There were at least two incidents of casualties in Thurnham during the Battle of Britain:

On 8 September 1940, a Hurricane aircraft, P3201, was shot down in enemy action over the Isle of Sheppey during an attack of Luftwaffe aircraft. Sub-lieutenant J C Carpenter of 46 Squadron baled out but was killed. His body was found by wardens in the vicinity of Green Pastures, Thurnham. He was based at Stapleford Tawney, Essex.[1]

On 15 September 1940, a Messerschmitt Bf109E, 2/JG53 crashed and burned at 12.45pm at Aldington Court Farm, Thurnham after combat with fighters. Lieutenant Rudolf Schmidt was killed. He was aged 24 and based at either Coquelles or Etaples. The Revd Arthur Scutt, vicar of St Mary's, Thurnham recorded the same day:[2]

> Much fighting over Thurnham during the Morning Service at 11am.

The air fights during the Battle of Britain were amongst the most important battles of the war. By 15 September 1940, the air war had reached a critical stage, later acknowledged to be the turning point of the whole war.[3] Although few realised it, Britain had begun to benefit from some cumulative effects. Despite suffering heavy bombing, the production rate for the aircraft factories was actually double that of Germany, so aircraft could be replaced at a reasonable rate.

Britain had the advantage of conducting air fights over home territory; any British pilot who baled out of a damaged aircraft over England without serious injury stood a good chance of rejoining the battle. A German pilot or air crew member who baled out was then captured as a prisoner of war so there was a steady reduction in their numbers.

Two of the aircraft extensively used by the Luftwaffe had serious limitations in aggressive combat: the Messerschmitt Bf109E had a combat radius of 125 miles. Although the aircraft could escort bombers to London, there was no spare fuel for extensive combat. The Zerstorer Bf110 was designed as a heavy fighter and carried five machine guns and two cannon, but it did not posses the rapid manoeuvrability that was needed in combat.[4]

On 15 September, a huge formation of aircraft gathered over France and came over to Britain. The German High Command believed that the British Fighter Command was so weakened that it could be finally defeated over London. At the end of the fighting it was estimated that 188 enemy aircraft were destroyed, 54 enemy aircraft were probably destroyed and 78 enemy aircraft were damaged. The air campaign faltered as the Luftwaffe crews began to suffer 'Kanalkrankheit': combat stress. Hitler hesitated for three days and then decided to postpone the invasion of Britain. 15 September 1940 later became known as Battle of Britain Day.[5]

Lieutenant Schmidt was buried in St Mary's churchyard, Thurnham on 18 September 1940.[6]

On 5 October 1961, a faculty was obtained to re-inter Lieutenant Schmidt.[7] His body was exhumed on 29 October 1962 and was re-interred at the German War Cemetery at Cannock Chase, Staffordshire.[8]

Appendix 2
Glossary of abbreviations used in original sources

1st **Air Mech**	Air Mechanic 1st class
A A D D	Anti Aircraft Defences Dover
A A Def	Anti Aircraft Defences
A B	Able Seaman
A B 2	Able Seaman 2nd Class
A C	Ammunition Column
A C W 2	Aircraft Woman 2nd Class
Agr Co	Agricultural Company
A M	Albert Medal
A Ord Corps	Army Ordnance Corps
A R C A	Associate of the Royal College of Arts
A R P	Air Raid Precautions
A S C	Army Service Corps
A T S	Auxiliary Territorial Service
A Vet. Corps	Army Veterinary Corps
Batt, Bn	Battalion
Bge	Brigade
Bty	Battery
B A O R	British Army of the Rhine
B E F	British Expeditionary Force
B S A P	British South African Police
C C 41	Civilian Clothing Control 1941 (Utility Mark)
C C S	Casualty Clearing Station
C M	Chief Mechanic
C M G	Companion of the Order of St. Michael and St. George
C M P	Corps of Military Police
C P O	Chief Petty Officer
C S	Colour Sergeant
Cmdr	Commander
Co	Company
C S M	Company Sergeant Major
Cyc	Cyclist
D A A G	Deputy Assistant Adjutant General
D A M S	Defensively Armed Merchant Ship
D C L I	Duke of Cornwall's Light Infantry
D C M	Distinguished Conduct Medal
D F M	Distinguished Flying Medal
D H	De Havilland
D M T	Divisional Motor Transport
Dr	Driver
D S O	Distinguished Service Order
Divl Emp Co	Divisional Employment Company
E K R	East Kent Regiment
E N S A	Entertainments National Service Association
F/A, F A	Field Ambulance
F/C	Field Company
Frtr Co	Fortress Company
F R S A	Fellow of the Royal Society of Arts
Gnr	Gunner
G A A S	*Not known*
G B D	General Base Depot
G C	George Cross
G H Q	General Headquarters
H C	Household Cavalry
H M A S	His Majesty's Australian Ship
H M M T B	His Majesty's Motor Torpedo Boat
H M S	His Majesty's Ship
H S Works Co	Home Service Works Company
H T Co	Horse Transport Company
I A	Indian Army
I E F	Indian Expeditionary Force
I W D, I W & D	Inland Waterways and Docks
I W T	Inland Water Transport
K C B	Knight Commander of the Order of the Bath
K O R L R	King's Own Royal Lancashire Regiment
K O Y L I	King's Own Yorkshire Light Infantry
K R R C	King's Royal Rifle Corps
L A A R	Light Anti Aircraft Regiment
L A C W	Leading Aircraft Woman
Ldg C C	*Not known*
Ldg S	Leading Seaman
Ldg Stkr	Leading Stoker
L D C	Local Defence Corps
L D V	Local Defence Volunteers
L I	Light Infantry
Lieut	Lieutenant
Lond. El. Eng	London Electrical Engineers
L of C	Lines of Communication

M Amb	Military Ambulance
M C	Military Cross
M G Corps (Cav)	Machine Gun Corps (Cavalry)
M G Gds	Machine Gun Guards
M M	Military Medal
M R	Mounted Regiment
M S M	Military Service Medal
M/T, MT	Mechanical Transport
N A A F I	Navy Army Air Forces Institute
N A D D	Naval Air Defence Dover
O S	Ordinary Seaman
Pte	Private
P O	Petty Officer
Q A O R H	Queen Alexandra's Own Royal Hussars
Q M A A C	Queen Mary's Army Auxiliary Corps
Q M S	Quartermaster Sergeant
Q O R W K R	The Queen's Own (Royal West Kent Regiment)
Res Sec	Reserve Section
Res of Off	Reserve of Officers
Road C Co	Road Corps Company
R A F	Royal Air Force
R A F A	Royal Air Force Association
R A F V R	Royal Air Force Volunteer Reserve
R A M C	Royal Army Medical Corps
R A S C	Royal Army Service Corps
R A V C	Royal Army Veterinary Corps
R B L	Royal British Legion
R D C	Royal Defence Corps
R D F	Royal Dublin Fusiliers
R E	Royal Engineers
R E M E	Royal Electrical and Mechanical Engineers
R F A	Royal Field Artillery
R F Aux	Royal Fleet Auxiliary
R F C	Royal Flying Corps
R F R	Royal Fleet Reserve
R G A	Royal Garrison Artillery
R H A	Royal Horse Artillery
R H Gds	Royal Horse Guards
R M	Royal Marines
R M C	Royal Medical Corps
R M Eng	Royal Marine Engineers
R M L I	Royal Marine Light Infantry
R N	Royal Navy
R N A S	Royal Naval Air Service
R N R	Royal Naval Reserve
R N V R	Royal Naval Volunteer Reserve
R O C	Royal Observer Corps
R S	Royal Signals
R S M	Regimental Sergeant Major
Spr	Sapper
Srgt	Sergeant
Sig	Signals
Stkr, Str	Stoker
S B R	Sick Berth Rating
S S	Steam Ship
S S M	Staff Sergeant Major
T B D	Torpedo Boat Division
T C	Tunnelling Corps
T F	Territorial Force
T M B	Trench Mortar Battery
T R Batt.	Training Reserve Battalion
T T O	*Not known*
U P S	University and Public Schools
V A D	Voluntary Aid Detachment
V B	Volunteer Brigade
V E	Victory in Europe
V J	Victory over Japan
V T C	Volunteer Training Corps
Wa T I Depot	*Not known*
W A A C	Women's Army Auxiliary Corps
W A A F	Women's Auxiliary Air Force
W I	Women's Institute
W R N S	Women's Royal Naval Service

Notes to the text

First World War: 1914 to 1919

1   Holy Cross Parish Magazine, Bearsted July 1917
        CKS Ref. P18/28/15

2   Holy Cross Parish Magazine, Bearsted February 1915
        CKS Ref. P18/28/14

3   I am indebted to David Barnes for this information and his useful website concerning research into the history of the Royal Flying Corps, Royal Naval Air Service and Royal Air Force. See Further Reading for website details.

4   Holy Cross Parish Magazine, Bearsted February 1916
        CKS Ref. P18/28/15

Bearsted and Thurnham during the First World War

1   No Return Tickets
        L Grace Dibble
        Stockwell Books 1989

2   Detling: a village in Kent
        C E Cornford
        Privately published, Lincoln 1980

3   *Ibid.* p.81

4   Album 2/13, Box E31
        Royal Engineers Library
        Brompton Barracks, Chatham

5   *Op.cit.* p.80
        C E Cornford

6 i   Sections 10.8.7 and 10.8.8
        Kent's Defence Heritage
        A Saunders, V Smith
        Kent County Council 1998

  ii pp. 69-86
        Kent Airfields in the Battle of Britain
        R J Brooks
        Meresborough Books 1981

7   *Op cit.* p.77
        C E Cornford

8   *Ibid.* p.61

9   *Ibid.*

10   *Op cit.* 69-86
        R J Brooks

11   p. 73
        Stockbury: A Stroll through the past
        Stockbury History Group 2004

12   K D 14,13
        Kent's Defence Heritage - Gazetteer
        A Saunders V Smith
        Kent County Council 1998

13 i p. 16
        Echoes from the Sky
        Richard N Scarth
        Hythe Civic Society 1999

  ii A photograph of the sound mirror under construction at Binbury is in the National Archives
        NA Ref. AIR1/121/15/40/105

14   *Op.cit.*
Richard N Scarth

15   Further information and a fuller description of the apparatus can be found on the website
www.doramusic.com/soundmirrors.htm

16   *Op.cit.* p.17
Richard N Scarth

17   *Op.cit., passim.*
www.doramusic.com/soundmirrors.htm

18   *Op.cit.* p.57-61, *passim.*
L Grace Dibble

Second World War: 1939 to 1945

1   pp. 115-116
A School at Bearsted
Kathryn Kersey
Privately published, Bearsted 2003

2   *Ibid.* p.205

3   *Ibid.*

4   Holy Cross Parish Magazine, Bearsted August 1945
CKS Ref. P18/28/20

Welcome Home: Second World War

1   Minutes of Welcome Home Fund 1945-1947
Bearsted and Thurnham Parish Council
CKS Ref. P18/29/9

2 - 4   *Ibid.*

War memorials in Bearsted and Thurnham

1   Few of the committee records are deposited at CKS.

2 - 3   *Op.cit.* p. 123
Kathryn Kersey

Appendix Battle of Britain casualties

1 i   p. 55
Aircraft Casualties in Kent, Part 1: 1939 to 1940
Compiled by G G Baxter, K A Owen and P Baldock
Meresborough Books 1990

ii   Entry for 8 September 1940
Battle of Britain Historical Society web site www. battleofbritain.net

2 i   *Op cit.* p. 60
Aircraft Casualties in Kent

ii   Private correspondence between Mr E H Clark and Michael Perring concerning R Schmidt burial dated 10 February 2005

3   Entry for 15 September 1940
Battle of Britain Historical Society web site www. battleofbritain.net

4   pp 97-112, *passim,*
The Royal Air Force
Michael Armitage 1993

5   *Ibid.* p97-112, *passim.*

6   *Op cit.* Private correspondence

7   Faculty re burial of German War dead, 5 October, 1961
CKS Ref. P369/6/7

8   *Op cit.* Private correspondence

Further reading

First World War

All Quiet on the Home Front – an oral history of life in Britain during the First World War
Richard Van Emden and Steve Humphries
Headline 2003

The British Army of August 1914
Ray Westlake
Spellmount Limited 2005

Defeat at Gallipoli
Nigel Steel and Peter Hart
Papermac 1995

Detling: a village in Kent
Mr C E Cornford
Privately published, Lincoln 1980
There is a copy in the Centre for Kentish Studies

Echoes from the Sky
Richard N Scarth
Hythe Civic Society 1999

Forgotten Voices of the Great War
Max Arthur
Ebury Press 2002

Old Contemptibles: the British Expeditionary Force in 1914
Robin Neilland
John Murray 2004

No Return Tickets
L Grace Dibble
Stockwell Books 1989

Over the Top: Great Battles of the First World War
Martin Marix Evans
Arcturus Publishing 2004

Tommy: the British Soldier in the First World War
Richard Holmes
Harper Collins 2003

The Wipers Times: a facsimile of the famous World War One trench newspaper
Introduced by Patrick Beaver
Papermac 1988

Second World War

Aircraft Casualties in Kent 1939-1940
G G Baxter and P Baldock
Meresborough Books 1990

Children into Exile
Peter Hayward
Buckland Publications 1997

Kent Airfields in the Second World War
Robin J Brooks
Countryside Books 1998

Kent at War
Bob Ogley
Froglet Publications 1994

The Phoney War on the Home Front
E S Turner
Michael Joseph 1961

Roof Over Britain – the official story of the anti-aircraft defences 1939-1942
His Majesty's Stationery Office 1943

The Royal Air Force - a history
Michael Armitage
Brockhampton 1993

Spitfire
Robert Jackson
Parragon 2003

Wartime Britain 1939-1945
Juliet Gardiner
Headline 2004

Internet Sites
There are many sites on the internet giving a great deal of information about both First and Second World Wars. They are worth exploring, particularly the Commonwealth War Graves site (www.cwgc.org.uk) and others giving details of individual regiments and medals awarded.

George Cross and Albert Medals: www.gc-database.co.uk

World War One Army organisation: www.warpath.orbat.com

Royal Flying Corps, the Royal Naval Air Service and the Royal Air Force: www.rfc.rnas-raf-register.org.uk

World War One aircraft: www.theaerodrome.com

Sound mirrors: www.doramusic.com/soundmirrors.htm

Battle of Britain: www.battleofbritain.net